Mabel B
Alexander's Sile

"Her face was the last he saw,
her hand the last he touched,
her voice the last he heard."

—from **Alexander Graham Bell
and the Conquest of Solitude**
by Robert Bruce

Mabel Bell

Bell

Alexander's Silent Partner

by Lilias M. Toward

Breton Books

Production Assistance: Bonnie Thompson
Composition: Glenda Watt
Fitzgerald Studio provided computerized photos from
the Alexander Graham Bell National Historic Park.
Mabel Bell: Alexander's Silent Partner is part of the
Large Print Program of the National Library of Canada.

Canadian Cataloguing in Publication Data

Toward, Lilias M.

> Mabel Bell

> Includes bibliographical references.
> Originally published: Methuen, 1984.
> ISBN 1-895415-11-X

1. Bell, Mabel Gardiner Hubbard, 1859-1923. 2. Bell,
Mabel Gardiner Hubbard, 1859-1923 — Correspon-
dence. 3. Deaf — United States — Biography. I. Bell,
Mabel Gardiner Hubbard, 1859-1923. II. Title.

HV2534.B44T68 1996   362.4'2'092   C96-950069-6

Contents

To my sister,
Helen MacDonald Rand

Introduction
by Hugh MacLennan

The author of this biography of an astonishing woman is herself a woman remarkable. Years had to pass before I realized this. We are cousins, and I have known Lilias from the age of five, which means that I never knew her at all until half of my life was over. One common bond we always had was a love of our native Cape Breton Island, which Lilias understands far better than I because for many years she made it her home.

Married to an Englishman in the late 1930s, she spent most of the war years in England, often in danger. She raised a son who is now an able and successful man in Canada. After her marriage dissolved, she returned to Nova Scotia, studied law, practiced it, and became a Q.C. She also planned and built a most unusual motel in the village of Baddeck and called it "The Silver Dart," its very design inspired by the airplane built by Alexander Graham Bell and his associates and named the *Silver Dart*. This was the first heavier-than-air machine to fly successfully in what then was known as the British Empire.

It was in Baddeck, where Lilias has lived on and off for many years, that she met Bell's daughter Marian Fairchild, widow of the distinguished American scientist Dr. David Fairchild. This lady asked Lilias to help her arrange the letters written to her by her mother over a period of thirty years, 1892-1922, the year in which Bell died and was buried on the grounds of his home Beinn Bhreagh, the beautiful mountain that overlooks the splendid expanse of

Baddeck Bay on the Bras d'Or Lakes. These letters form the basis of Lilias Toward's book, which is virtually a biography of Mabel Bell and her husband.

Alexander Graham Bell and his wife were children of the mid-Victorian Age, and they lived on into the twentieth century. Like most Victorians, they had little historical perspective of this astonishing epoch of which they were prime products.

Lytton Strachey wrote of that time that it was "an age in which everything was discovered and nothing was known." An overstatement, of course, but a suggestive one. I would prefer to amend Strachey's sentence into, "An age in which its most dynamic people learned prodigiously how to manipulate material nature without thinking it necessary to understand the essential nature of Man himself." Even a man as shrewd as Mark Twain took it for granted that the domination of nature by mechanical devices was certain to produce a Golden Age in which humanity would at last rise to its full stature.

In such a tiime—indeed, well into our own century—inventors were presented to school children as heroes and supermen, and it was assumed almost without question that material progress would result in an enormous human happiness. As we all know, this dream ended in 1914. Toward the end of his life the greatest inventor of them all, Thomas Edison, remarked grimly that he had never met a happy man. Even sadder was the disillusionment of Alfred Nobel. When he invented dynamite, he had the sincere hope that it would be a blessing to mankind because it would eliminate much of the brutal pick and shovel work required for construction. To his horror, dynamite was immediately grabbed by the armies and put into high-explosive shells. So at the end of his life, Nobel turned over much of his wealth to the Novel Prizes, of which the most famous, and certainly the most forlorn, is the Peace Prize.

But there were two other aspects of the Victorian Age that were not dominated by power-lust and greed. One was the development of the art of the healer; the other was the struggle for the emancipation of women.

In this story of Mabel Bell's life, as revealed by Lilias Toward, these latter two elements in the Victorian epoch come together; literally, they married each other. For Bell's famous invention was to a considerable extent a by-product of the life work of his father and himself, the teaching of what he called "visible speech." Had not Bell studied so meticulously the workings of the human ear, he would not have invented the telephone, which someone else would have discovered if he had not. Indeed, in the biographical section of *Larousse*, Bell is described as "*un des inventeurs du téléphone (1876).*" That it was a beneficent invention is beyond serious question. When my mother was a very old lady living in Halifax, while I was in Montreal, I used to call her up twice a week and she used to say, "God bless Alexander Graham Bell."

But this book is largely about Bell's wife and helpmate, Mabel.

One of the scourges of the time before antibiotics was scarlet fever. I remember as a child passing houses in quarantine with signs reading SCARLET FEVER on their doors. Generally the patient recovered with no harm done, but in many cases partial or total deafness resulted.

At the age of five, Mabel Hubbard, daughter of a

ix

distinguished man in Massachusetts, caught scarlet fever and became totally deaf. Her father toured Europe, consulting scientists in the hope of finding a cure, and finally he encountered in Boston the young Scottish immigrant Alexander Bell. Bell taught her to converse in visible speech about the most abstruse subjects. Moreover, he fell in love with her, and after a number of years she married him and became a true and extremely useful partner in all his subsequent work.

With the Kennan family, the Bells discovered Cape Breton and Baddeck, and it was on the mountain he called Beinn Bhreagh that they spent much of the last thirty years of their lives.

Reading my cousin's book brought me a deep feeling of nostalgia for the Cape Breton of my childhood, before the new highways were built and the quickest way to reach Baddeck from Sydney was by the old paddlewheeler *Marion*, which left her dock at 7:00 A.M. and generally reached Baddeck in the mid-afternoon. The *Marion* sailed down Sydney harbor, often got caught in heavy seas when she rounded Point Aconi, then passed into the tranquil and beautiful fjord which is the Bras d'Or lake. She put in at every little wharf along the route, taking on passengers and putting them off, and many of her passengers were sheep, cattle and chickens in cages. There was always a great excitement when she entered Baddeck Bay and passed under the lee of Bell's famous home, and even a little child knew that a great man was living and working there, though at the time he did not know that the invention he was producing was the hydrofoil.

June 1984

Preface
by Lilias M. Toward

Over twenty years have passed since I first realized what a remarkable woman Mrs. Alexander Graham Bell had been. At that time her daughter, the late Marian H. Fairchild, asked me to help arrange the letters her mother had written to her between 1892 and 1922. I found them fascinating, capturing in an informal but immediate way all that went on at Beinn Bhreagh during that period.

But this was only one side of her life, and I longed to read her other letters. These were in the Bell Room at the Hubbard Memorial Library, part of the National Geographic Society headquarters in Washington. Copies of many of these letters were loaned to the Alexander Graham Bell National Historic Park in Baddeck, Nova Scotia, by the family of the late Dr. Gilbert H. Grosvenor, her son-in-law.

Shortly after her mother's death in 1910, when she was going through her papers, Mabel wrote:

I do not desire that my letters be burnt unread. If any of my descendants are interested enough to wade through them, they are at liberty to do so. I personally cannot bear to destroy letters which are the record of a life and would never willingly do so.

From the many bound volumes of letters and journals I have selected those that I felt would best portray "the record of a life." For some of the background material I have referred to the *Beinn Bhreagh Recorder*, the *A.E.A. Bulletin* and the *Home Notes*. These are bound volumes gathered by Bell primarily for use by his associates and are now available at the Alexander Graham Bell National Historic Park.

Dr. G.H. Grosvenor, writing to Miss Mary Blatchford, a cousin of Mrs. Bell's, on July 25, 1923, made this comment regarding his mother-in-law: "Mr. Bell's fame is secure for all ages but few know the quality and genius of his wife, one of the greatest minds and personalities of the times." It seems timely to let Mabel Gardiner Hubbard Bell tell her own story through her letters. Although completely deaf from the age of five, she was able to lead a remarkably full and unusually inspiring life as the wife of Alexander Graham Bell, one of the great inventors of his age.

Mabel was born in 1857 and brought up in Cambridge, Massachusetts, in a cultured home by remarkable parents. Her father, Gardiner Greene Hubbard, a distinguished Boston and Washington attorney, was keenly interested in matters pertaining to the public welfare. His father, the Honorable Samuel Hubbard, had been a justice of the Massachusetts Supreme Court and his mother the daughter of Gardiner Greene who, in his day, was reputed to be one of the wealthiest men in Boston.

In the mid-1850s Gardiner Hubbard organized the Cambridge Horse Railroad Company, the first such service in the country outside of New York City. He and his associates were also responsible for obtaining a water supply system for Cambridge, and he organized the Cambridge Gas Light Company. The president of the United States appointed him chairman of a special committee to make recommendations on the possibility of delivering mail across the country by railroad.

Mabel lost her hearing from scarlet fever in 1863 when she was five. At a time when deaf children, if educated at all, were segregated in asylums for deaf mutes, Mabel received her education at home with hearing children. First her mother and then her inspired teacher, Mary True, preserved her speech and taught her lip reading, a practice generally unheard of at that time. When she attended a private school at the age of twelve, she was placed in classes with hearing children two and three years her senior—an indication not only of Mabel's great intellectual ability, but also of her mother and Miss True's success in educating her.

After his daughter lost her hearing, in addition to his other activities Mr. Hubbard devoted a great deal of time to encouraging the teaching of speech to the deaf. He helped establish the Clarke School for the Deaf in Northampton, Massachusetts, and became its first president. With friends he formed the National Geographic Society and was its first president. He was also a regent of the Smithsonian Institution. His wide circle of friends included many of the most distinguished men in the country.

Mrs. Hubbard, a deeply religious woman who learned Hebrew in order to read the Bible in its original language, shared her husband's many interests and friends.

Like her mother, Mabel was fortunate in her marriage. Alexander Graham Bell was not only a distinguished inventor, but had gained a great reputation for his work for the deaf. He understood, as few people could, the problems facing deaf people.

Bell's achievements as an inventor and in his work

for the deaf have been recognized throughout the world. Nowhere is this more evident than in the Alexander Graham Bell National Historic Park at Baddeck, Nova Scotia. The historic park, located within a few miles of Beinn Bhreagh where Bell lived a part of each year for more than thirty-five years, is operated by Parks Canada. It contains many photographs taken by Bell's son-in-law, Dr. G.H. Grosvenor, for the National Geographic Society showing Dr. Bell and his various activities while living in the area. In many, Mabel is at his side. Visitors to the museum cannot help but sense that her constant companionship played an important part in his achievements. She was a leader in progressive education, establishing the first Montessori school in Canada at her home near Baddeck in 1912.

Hers was the vision to risk investing a legacy of $20,000—a considerable fortune in 1908—in an idea, but Mabel Bell believed that her husband's experiments relating to aeronautics could lead to a heavier-than-air flying machine. Not only did she believe in them; she made them possible. She organized and financed an association of four young men to work with Bell, and together they turned their dreams into reality. They were the first to discover, describe and apply the fundamental principles of all practical biplane construction.

Mrs. Fairchild once told me that one of her mother's outstanding qualities was that of a creative listener. At mealtime it was not unusual for family and guests alike to thump the tabletop in an effort to attract her attention so that they might have the joy of sharing some particular interest with her. It was this gift that made her indispensable to her husband during their forty-five years of marriage. She was always at hand to watch an experiment, always ready to sit up half the night talking things over with him and to encourage him in overcoming difficulties.

Many books have been written about the life of Alexander Graham Bell, and in many of them reference is made to his wife. Here, for the first time, is Mabel Bell's own story, told primarily through her letters to her husband and to other relatives and friends.

Acknowledgements

This book would never have been written if the late Marian H. Fairchild had not shared with me the letters she received from her mother over a period of thirty years. For the other side of Mabel Bell's life I am grateful to the family of the late Dr. Gilbert H. Grosvenor. They placed the extensive collection of material pertaining to Dr. and Mrs. Bell, and gathered by Dr. Grosvenor over many years, in the Alexander Graham Bell National Historic Park in Baddeck, Nova Scotia. It was Mr. J.W. Stephens, superintendent of that national park, who made me aware of the existence of this material and encouraged me to make use of it.

Dr. Alexander Graham Bell Fairchild and his wife Alva read my manuscript and made helpful suggestions, as did Marjory Whitelaw and Kim Rutherford. Elsie Collins gave loyal and indefatigable assistance. This book owes much to Tony Foster.

1
Early Childhood

ON A JANUARY DAY IN 1863, a beautifully dressed young mother holding her little girl by the hand boarded a train for New York in the Boston railway station. Gertrude Hubbard was fulfilling a birthday promise to her daughter Mabel, and they were on their way to visit her parents, Mr. and Mrs. Robert McCurdy.

The little girl was the second of four daughters, and although her name was Mabel Gardiner, she was often called May by her family. For her fifth birthday, on November 25, 1862, Mabel had been promised that she could travel with her mother the next time she went to New York. That day had come, and Mabel was so excited she could hardly contain herself. A winsome little girl of unusual intelligence, she had lovely fair skin, gray-blue eyes and silky light-brown hair worn parted in the middle, giving her a surprising air of maturity.

Shortly after their arrival in New York, Mabel contracted scarlet fever. For weeks her mother and grandparents hovered over her fearing she would die. When the crisis passed she lay without speaking, completely unresponsive to her surroundings. The doctors warned Mrs. Hubbard that her child's intellect might have been damaged by the disease. Eventually, her anxious mother noticed that although Mabel's eyes followed her movements she still did not speak. A few weeks before, Mabel had been taken to the Barnum Exhibition to see Tom Thumb and his tiny wife. So fascinated was she by these midgets that her mother bought her a picture of them. She brought it with her to New York to show her grandparents. Mrs. Hubbard picked up the picture and showed it to Mabel, who murmured, "little lady." These were the first words she had spoken in six weeks. Mrs. Hubbard understood suddenly that, although her daughter's mind was perfectly clear, Mabel was completely deaf.[1]

When Mr. and Mrs. Hubbard realized that Mabel would never hear again, they sought every scrap of information on how to educate a deaf child. As a member of the Massachusetts State Board of Education, Hubbard had contacts all over the New England states in the field of education. Everyone told him that it was impossible to teach a deaf child to speak, or even if it were possible, that it would be undesirable because of the peculiar harsh quality of the voice. He was told that soon Mabel would lose what speech she had. Indeed, there existed a general belief that being mute was part of the affliction of deafness in young children.

The principal of the Hartford School for Deaf Mutes assured Hubbard that nothing could be done to educate deaf children until they reached the age of eleven. They could then be sent to an asylum for deaf mutes to be taught sign language. In his visits to these various asylums Hubbard had met children weirdly silent—their only means of communication by strange baffling gestures. He could not bear to think of Mabel being brought up like that, condemned to a life of isolation, cut off from family and friends.

In the midst of this despair he learned that Dr.

Howe, of the Perkins Institute for the Blind in Boston, had visited schools for the deaf in Germany some years before where he found deaf children being taught to speak. Hubbard went to see Dr. Howe, who explained that prior to the nineteenth century there were only three schools for the deaf in the world: in Germany, France and Scotland. The Braidwood School in Scotland had developed a method of teaching speech to the deaf. Their system promised to be a model for teaching the deaf in America.

John Braidwood, the grandson of Thomas Braidwood, founder of the Scottish school, came to America in 1812 and established a school for the deaf in Virginia. Unfortunately, his school was doomed to failure. Braidwood was an alcoholic.

The Reverend Thomas Gallaudet, who wanted to establish a school for the deaf in Hartford, Connecticut, went to Scotland looking for assistance. He had hoped to use their oral method of teaching, but those in charge refused to reveal their system; they suggested contacting John Braidwood in America. Knowing of Braidwood's affliction, Gallaudet wanted nothing to do with him. Instead, he went to France where he learned the use of a sign language devised by Abbé de l'Epée that the French had adopted for teaching deaf children. He returned to America and in 1817 established the Hartford School for Deaf Mutes, using sign language as the basis of instruction. Braidwood's oral system was used for a time in one or two small schools, but as most of the teachers for the deaf in America were trained at the Hartford School for Deaf Mutes, it was eventually replaced by the sign language method.[2]

Encouraged by his meeting with Dr. Howe, Hubbard

sent to Germany for reports, school books and other educational aids. He learned that in Germany the speech of children who had once spoken was being carefully preserved and made the basis of their subsequent education. With suitable home care such children need never become mute.

When Mrs. Hubbard learned of this, she became determined to preserve her child's speech. She persisted in talking to Mabel as though she could hear, and Mabel talked and played with her sisters and their friends as naturally as if she could hear. Mrs. Hubbard wisely insisted that if Mabel made signs, the whole family must ignore them and force her to speak.

This constant use of spoken language prevented Mabel from forgetting the words she knew, and her mother ingeniously devised means to stimulate the recollection of words that were half forgotten. She insisted that the little girl watch her lips as she spoke, so that in time Mabel was able to read the lips of people she saw frequently.

Mrs. Lippitt, wife of the governor of Rhode Island, had a daughter, Jennie, who had also lost her hearing from scarlet fever. Mrs. Lippitt had succeeded in saving her daughter's speech and in teaching her to lip read. She provided great encouragement to Mrs. Hubbard when they met. The two mothers had much in common and encouraged each other in what was generally considered to be an impossible undertaking.

Jennie was a few years older than Mabel and had been receiving instruction for a longer time. By watching her progress Mrs. Hubbard realized the importance of reading as a means of increasing the vocabulary of a deaf child. Regardless of whether or not the child understands what is read, it is an effective way of presenting words to the eye of the deaf child in much the same way that a hearing child has unfamiliar words directed to the ear.[3]

In the autumn of 1864 a Miss Conklin was engaged as governess in the Hubbard home with the responsibility of teaching Mabel to read. She also taught Mabel's two younger sisters, Roberta, whom they called Berta, and Grace, as well as a neighbouring child, Carrie Dwyer, for Mrs. Hubbard believed it important that Mabel's school life should be shared with normal hearing children.

Miss Conklin was an attractive and pleasant young woman, but not particularly interested in teaching. Would she be sufficiently stimulating to interest Mabel? Mrs. Hubbard, pregnant at the time, was glad to rely on Miss Conklin for Mabel's care; for in addition to her deafness, the scarlet fever had affected Mabel's sense of equilibrium. She had to learn to balance by sight, but in the dark was apt to fall unless someone held her hand.

After the baby, Marian, was born in April 1865, the Hubbards went on a trip through the White Mountains looking for a suitable summer place to take their family while extensive repairs were being made to their house on Brattle Street in Cambridge. They came to the village of Bethel, Maine, and engaged rooms for their family for July in the home of Dr. Nathanial P. True. When they returned in July, they met Dr. True's young daughter Mary, who had just finished training as a teacher. A delightful, whimsical woman of twenty-one, she had a turned-up nose and eyes sparkling with fun.

Mary True was happy to be sharing her home with this charming family. Hubbard, a tall, distinguished-looking gentleman then in his early forties, wore gold-rimmed glasses and a long fair beard. His wife was very beautiful. A deep rich voice added to her charm. In the Hubbard family the oldest daughter, Gertrude, named after her mother and grandmother, was always referred to as "Sister." Almost sixteen the summer they came to Bethel, she appeared very much the young lady and was apt to laugh at Mabel, eight years her junior, in her assumption of dignity toward "the children"—meaning Berta and Grace, who were only six and four, and the baby Marian.

Mary True soon made friends with everyone, but was drawn particularly to Mabel, who played so much by herself and welcomed the companionship of "Miss Rue," as she called her new friend.

Before the family left Bethel it was understood that Miss Conklin would not be continuing as governess. Miss True was asked if she would come to Cambridge and teach the three little sisters and their friend until such time as a trained teacher of the deaf could be found for Mabel. She arrived on October 24, 1865, and quickly adapted to the life of the Hubbard family, embarking on her teaching duties with enthusiasm.

Mrs. Hubbard and Mary True often compared notes on their method of teaching Mabel not only to speak but also to understand language, for they had nothing but their own intuition to guide them. Mrs. Hubbard recalled the long hard effort to get Mabel to repeat the 23rd Psalm, "The Lord Is My Shepherd." A visitor to their home could not believe that this little deaf child had any conception of the meaning of the words she was repeating and asked her what a shepherd was. Much to her mother's chagrin, Mabel promptly replied: "Oh, I know, it's the man who takes the poor little lambs to the butcher's."

Mary True found Berta, Grace and Carrie Dwyer easy enough to teach once she had their attention, but formal lessons left Mabel confused and uncertain. For a time she simply played with her. She told her endless stories, invented word games and took her on walks around Cambridge, making games of showing her how to pay her fare on the streetcar or going into a shop to purchase material for the next day's lesson. They went to the state legislature where she attempted to explain its significance. On their return home they always retraced their day's outing on a map.

Writing later in life about her experiences in teaching Mabel, Miss True said she never tried to give her information; it had to be deduced from the language Mabel already knew. She looked for some fact or happening to clinch a lesson, to put into use a word or phrase that could be explained only by context. She would start from a fact or subject and by questions and suggestions lead up to whatever she wanted to explain in such a way that Mabel understood the word or phrase as necessary to the sense. Miss True couldn't exactly explain how she did it, but together they read page upon page of the school reader, using words or phrases Mabel already knew to explain unfamiliar ones. Sometimes the language was queer and the definition crude, but somehow she progressed. Miss True taught her grammar after the old style of parsing. She learned the various parts of speech: nouns, pronouns, verbs, adjectives, conjunctions and prepositions. Parsing taught her the relationship of words and their value in a sentence. From Miss True's explanation of conjunctions

Mabel was able to say: "Oh yes, a conjunction is like an isthmus, it joins the peninsula to the mainland."[4]

As Hubbard watched his wife and Mary True teach Mabel to speak and understand the speech of others, he thought of all the other children in the various asylums he had visited and wondered if the same miracle could be wrought for them. Evening after evening, sitting by the library fire, he discussed the problem with Mrs. Hubbard. At length he exclaimed, "The day will come when every deaf child in America will be taught to speak."[5] Having conceived such an idea, he promptly set out to do something about it, organizing a movement to stimulate public interest in the education of the deaf.

Such a goal was not achieved without having to overcome obstacles. In 1864 he attempted to persuade the Massachusetts legislature to grant a charter for the establishment of a school for teaching very young deaf children to speak. The attempt failed, partly because the country was torn by civil war, but chiefly because of strong opposition by the directors of the Hartford School for Deaf Mutes.

His next attempt resulted in the establishment of a small school as an example of what could be done. It opened in June 1866 at Chelmsford with five pupils under the direction of Miss Harriet B. Rogers, a specially trained teacher. Mabel was not enrolled. She was doing very well under Mary True, and her mother insisted that she should associate with hearing children. But people around Boston were becoming aware of the Chelmsford School through the efforts of Mrs. Josiah Quincy, who invited members of Boston society, including several members of the legisla-

8

ture, to her home to see for themselves what Miss Rogers had accomplished with her pupils.

The following year Hubbard again petitioned the legislature for a school charter. When he called on the governor he learned that a Mr. John Clarke of Northampton had offered to provide $50,000 if the state of Massachusetts would found a school for deaf children in his city. Mr. Clarke suffered from deafness and was concerned that deaf children should be educated. Hubbard was delighted at the idea that Massachusetts was about to found such a school; he realized, however, that sign language advocates would be lobbying the legislature to adopt their system. How could he convince the legislators to adopt the oral method instead?

The success of Miss Rogers had become well known, and he could rely on her to testify. As an able attorney he appreciated the importance of good witnesses to help win his case. Who would be better than his own little daughter and her teacher, Miss True? It was not easy for the young lady from Bethel to stand before a special committee of the Massachusetts legislature and explain to them how she had accomplished something that many of the most respected people in the country said was impossible. But she did it.

Then Hubbard explained to Mabel that the gentlemen were meeting to decide whether to build a real school for her friend Miss Rogers and that she could help by answering any questions they might wish to ask. Seated in the great chair before the committee she was an alert, appealing child. Never having known isolation, and belonging to a family with many friends and relatives, she was neither embarrassed nor shy before these strange gentlemen. Although her voice was not normal or perfect, it was intelligible. After a little hesitation, the gentlemen took Hubbard's advice and plied her with questions in history, geography and simple arithmetic, which Mabel answered promptly and with enthusiasm.[6]

On the recommendation of this special committee, the legislature enacted two bills. One granted a charter for the establishment of the Clarke Institution for Deaf Mutes at Northampton (later called the Clarke School for the Deaf); the other provided for the teaching of deaf children from five to ten years of age at Clarke or other schools for the deaf in the state of Massachusetts, with funds to be provided by the state. In all such schools the children were to be taught to speak and lip read.

When the Clarke Institution for Deaf Mutes was incorporated in 1867, Hubbard was its first president, and he continued in that office until 1877. Throughout his life he maintained a great interest in the school.

When summer came Miss True took Mabel home with her to Bethel. But her happy days in Maine were brought to a sudden close when a letter arrived from Mrs. Hubbard informing them that baby Marian had died after a brief illness. Mabel was heartbroken. Miss True led her to a huge tree at the far end of the orchard, and together they climbed to their favorite branch from which they could examine the blue sky through the green leaves. Gathering Mabel on her lap, Mary tried explaining the significance of death and of heaven. But the years never entirely erased from Mabel's memory the recollection of that first grief.[7]

2
Childhood in Europe

BY AUTUMN 1869 the Hubbards were confident that Mabel would fit into a regular private school. She was sent to Miss Songer's school where her sisters were already enrolled. That same year the Boston school board started the Horace Mann School for the Deaf, and it was arranged that Miss True should teach there. This abrupt change of lifestyle might have been very difficult for both Mabel and Mary True had not Mrs. Hubbard suggested that Mary continue living with them. In order not to undermine her independence, she suggested that Mary might help Mabel with her lessons after school. Help was needed. In the larger classes Mabel could not always watch her teacher's face.

In the summer of 1870 Hubbard set off with his family for Europe, and although he returned home the following October, Mrs. Hubbard and her daughters remained abroad until August 1873. Before leaving for home he arranged for Mabel to attend a day school in Vienna run by Herr and Frau Lehfeld. He invited Miss Harriet Rogers, principal of the Clarke Institution for Deaf Mutes, to come to Vienna and live with Mabel to improve her own teaching techniques by studying the German method of teaching the deaf. Berta and Grace were placed in a private school in Switzerland, while Mrs. Hubbard and Sister planned to live in Paris for the winter.

Writing in her journal on September 2, 1871, a fourteen-year-old Mabel described the arrangements:

When I came in Mama's room, I found her waiting to speak to me. She began very guardedly but I saw at once the end. It was for me to go to Vienna for the winter. "I know what you mean but I won't go." Mama said she only wanted me to think about it. I was to do as I pleased in the matter. They thought that if I went there, I would learn German more thoroughly and that it would be much to my improvement; it would help me to speak and understand much better and faster and besides Cousin Copley and Cousin Mary would be there as well as Miss Rogers, who would stay at the same house with me. I might go to Rome in the spring. The children would go to a boarding school in Geneva and Mama and Sister would hover between us.

On the whole I think I had better go to Vienna for Mama says it concerns my future welfare. I will try and decide like Charles V of Germany and see if after all "I may not be glad afterwards."[1]

This was the period, not long after the close of the Civil War, when so many New Englanders who were unable to adapt to changed social conditions turned their back on America and went to Europe. Some, like Henry James, who depicted these people so vividly in his novels, never returned. Others stayed for extended visits; Mrs. Hubbard and her family remained three years. Mabel described the kind of life these roving Americans led:

We stayed two weeks in Geneva and last Friday the children went to boarding school. We visited them and I would have enjoyed staying there for the summer only not particularly as a scholar for I am almost

afraid of the many strange faces and the stares people give me when I speak.

At Montreaux we met Cousins Carrie and Mary Blatchford. The same day Auntie Bertie and Cousin Lizzie Greene arrived at the hotel opposite our pension. Auntie left on Thursday but I shall see her again at Wien for she is going to Constantinople and it is all decided that I am to spend three or four months at Herr Lehfeld's school. I am to leave Mama in a fortnight and proceed to Vienna by way of Munich with Papa. I cannot go to Venice for our new clothes have taken up all of Papa's money.[2]

During the winter in Vienna, Mabel was far too busy to miss anyone except her mother, to whom she wrote long letters describing her life at school. In her free time she and Miss Rogers explored the churches and art galleries.

She had become an appealing girl. So much so that Buba, a Hungarian-Hebrew boy a year or so older who also attended the school, had become attracted to her; Mabel wrote her mother:

I don't suppose you would like to have a gentleman of whom you know scarcely anything tuck you under the chin, pat your face, it is different with the others who wouldn't dare to be so familiar. If they were, Buba would be sure to scold them, for it seems he will let only himself play with me.[3]

In spite of such familiarity, Buba was the most important person in her school life. She told her father that she enjoyed school because she was doing as well as Buba. She found her lessons in speech the most difficult, but seldom left the classroom feeling she had been stupid.

However, as she confided to her mother, there were times when she didn't do very well:

I did not have very good lessons this morning but after relearning them, I got them very well without mistakes. Buba did not seem to have much better lessons and I was much pleased as it is nicer to have somebody as bad as I than to be alone. Buba is just as usual only sometimes too familiar which I decidedly don't like. I don't mind Herr Lehfeld's tucking me under the chin, but it's not so with Buba. I consider it something short of a personal insult.

Herr Lehfeld told me a new little boy was coming in a week or so. His name is Michael and he is six or seven. I hope he will be very timid, delicate and gentle and will love me dearly. It would be so nice.[4]

In letters to both her father and mother, she asked for newspapers. She wrote that Miss Rogers received papers from Northampton but they were so full of details of the great fire in Boston that she got tired reading about it, and then added: "But I wish those papers would tell me more about Europe. I really don't know if the Queen of England is dead or alive; if Napoleon is Emperor or not and that vexes me very much."[5]

Sometimes Mabel disliked the strenuous routine of her life in Vienna. She enjoyed school but wished she didn't have to get up so early and have quite so much to do. Nor was she happy to be dragged out of a warm room on every holiday and taken to see something. Yet, when she and Miss Rogers visited the art galleries, she studied the pictures carefully and later described them in her journal: "Above, resting in a reclining attitude on a cloud, was God.

14

He had a long gray beard and gray mantle. I don't like to see him thus represented. No one knows that he is an old man."[6]

Mabel notes in her journal that her mother and Sister have gone to Rome where they are joined by her grandparents, Mr. and Mrs. McCurdy, then adds: "I feel sometimes so forgotten here among these rough boys (and girls) and wish April was almost here."[7] In January she was elated to learn that she and Miss Rogers were to leave Vienna about the first of March instead of April to join her mother and Sister in Rome.

Like many of the adult members of the international colony living in Rome, Mabel was intrigued by royalty. She read of the National Thanksgiving in St. Paul's, London, for the recovery of the Prince of Wales and wrote in her journal: "I only hope 'England's oldest son' will prove himself worthy of this."[8]

After his recovery the Prince and Princess of Wales came to Rome, where they attended service in the English Chapel and were observed very carefully by the little American girl:

Sunday morning was very unpleasant but nevertheless we went to the English Chapel hoping to see the Prince and Princess of Wales. We were successful and I liked them very much but I did not think the former very devout because at prayers when I looked up for a moment from my prayer book, I saw him turn his head all the way around in a way that reminded me of a naughty little boy. I was told some things about him which one of the Ladies of Honor told Mrs. Randolf, an American lady who lives downstairs. She says that he, the Prince, has only common sense, hates learning

15

and all that sort of thing, but he is so kind and generous that all who have any dealing with him love him. He loves his wife, Princess Alexandra, very much and is kind and loving to her instead of being just the opposite as the American papers say. He is very short and bald. His hair and whiskers are very light. I could not see the Princess very well but that afternoon the Princess of Piedmont took the English Princess out for a drive in a state carriage with an outrider in a livery of scarlet trimmed with gold. I could not see the Princess of Piedmont, but I liked the English Princess. She sat very upright which I liked, but I thought she ought to have dressed up more. She wore a purple dress and bonnet, the same as she had on in the morning church.[9]

Mabel had matured during these years in Europe; in her journal she described their visit to the Pope:

I am so tall and look so old that Mama was afraid they would think me too old to be allowed to wear a colored dress, so as I had no black dress of my own, she loaned me her dress. Didn't I feel fine! They say I looked twenty years old.[10]

Early in May, they left Rome for Florence. There they were joined by Berta and Grace from their school in Switzerland. Although constantly on the move, Mrs. Hubbard always arranged for teachers so that her daughters' education should not be neglected. Mabel described this life:

Our drawing teacher came this morning and we learned to draw heads. Our regular teacher is very sick now so that we have no school. Yesterday morning we all went to the Corsini Palace to the large gallery there. Our teacher is ill with some infectious disease.

Of course, we are not sick now, but the doctor says that the illness seldom shows itself till it is eight days since it began. Tomorrow will be the eighth day since we saw her and we shall see. I have very little fear for myself. It has not been my good fortune to be confined longer than one whole day in bed since that fever which deprived me of my hearing.

As I grow older, I feel my loss more severely. At home I don't remember the idea ever entering my head to wish to hear, but here where I am thrown more into the society of strangers, I feel somewhat discontented. Only somewhat, thank God. I am getting to understand more strangers without help.[11]

Mabel's time in Europe ended with several months in Paris and a visit to England as the guest of her father's friends, Lord and Lady Willoughby Jones.

3
Mabel's Encounter with Bell

THREE GENERATIONS OF THE BELL FAMILY were students and teachers of speech. Early in the nineteenth century Alexander Graham Bell's grandfather, Alexander Bell, had made himself a recognized authority on pure diction; he was a teacher of speech in London and an author of a textbook on elocution. His son Melville became his assistant, then fell in love with Eliza Grace Symonds of Edinburgh. Although partially deaf from the age of ten, she was a gifted artist and musician. The young couple were married and settled in Edinburgh where Melville became a professor of elocution. During their time in Edinburgh three sons were born; the second, Alexander Graham Bell, was born on March 3, 1847.

At the age of fourteen Alexander was sent to London to live with his grandfather, who supervised his education. Thinking the boy—whose only ambition was to be a concert pianist—rather indolent, the elder Alexander set out to improve him. He made certain that he learned Latin, became well read and even saw that he was fitted out with what he considered proper city clothes.

Occasionally, out of loneliness—for he had no companions his own age in London—young Alexander attended his grandfather's speech classes. In time he became familiar with the older Bell's teaching methods and his curiosity was aroused. In later years he looked back on the time spent with his grandfather as the turning point in his life.

When he returned to Edinburgh he found it difficult to accept the restrictions of being a schoolboy. The pocket money that his grandfather had allowed him was discontinued by his father. But his mind was made up. Teaching, he decided, would become his life's work. He applied for and obtained a teaching position as a pupil-teacher in Elgin on Scotland's rugged east coast. He remained there a year before returning to take Latin and Greek at Edinburgh University. At age seventeen, he went back to Elgin as a teacher of elocution and music.

When the elder Bell died in 1865, Alexander's father moved to London and took over his classes, eventually becoming a recognized authority in speech training. Bell's *Standard Elocutionist* ran into many editions throughout England and America. Besides producing this internationally recognized publication, Melville Bell spent twenty years in search of an acceptable universal alphabet.

He discovered that for all individuals the mechanism of speech is uniform when producing the same sound. He developed symbols to indicate how the tongue and lips should be placed to pronounce any given sound. The system proved useful in teaching foreign languages. He called it "visible speech."

It never occurred to Melville that visible speech might be useful in teaching the deaf to speak until it was suggested by Miss Susannah E. Hull, a teacher of the deaf in London. By this time young Alexander had moved to London. Melville sent his son to Miss Hull's school to instruct her and the staff in the Bell system. Alexander immediately realized its possibilities. His ambition fired, he decided to devote his life to the training of teachers of the deaf in the use of visible speech.[1] He attended University College in London for a few months and began working privately with deaf pupils.

Tragedy struck the Bell family during these years. Two sons died of tuberculosis. Alexander suffered such grief that his health was affected. As a young man, Melville had gone to Newfoundland for his health. He decided now to leave London and emigrate to Canada for his son's sake. They arrived in Quebec on August 1, 1870, and traveled to

Paris, Ontario, to stay with friends. Later, they bought a home on Tutelo Heights, four miles from Brantford.

Some months later Melville went to lecture at the Lowell Institute in Boston. While there he was invited to give a further series of lectures for the benefit of teachers of deaf children. As he had already accepted a teaching engagement in Canada, he recommended his son take his place. Alexander arrived in Boston on April 1, 1871, and during the next year gave lectures at various schools for the deaf in the vicinity and taught deaf pupils privately.

Hubbard had returned from Europe in the autumn of 1871. He went to Northampton, Massachusetts, to report to the board of governors and staff of the Clarke Institution for Deaf Mutes on all that he had learned about schools for the deaf in Europe. He met Alexander Graham Bell, who was giving a course of lectures on visible speech, and came to the conclusion that the young man had great empathy with the deaf combined with an unusual degree of understanding of the difficulties deaf children encounter in life.

When Alexander returned home to Brantford, he resumed his experiments with tuning forks that he had begun in Scotland. Hour after hour in the little drawing-room at Tutelo Heights he sang a single note into the piano, his foot on the pedal, listening for the answering vibration of the corresponding key. Not surprisingly, friends and neighbors considered him a little peculiar, but he was oblivious to them. The harmonic or multiple telegraph was beginning to take shape in his mind.

In October 1872, Bell returned to Boston and opened a school for the correction of stammering and other speech defects. He also undertook the education of George Sanders, the young son of a prominent Haverhill businessman who had been born deaf. The following year Bell became professor of vocal physiology at Boston University. His spare time was spent experimenting on his multiple telegraph.

Mrs. Hubbard and her daughters did not return from Europe until the summer of 1873. In the meantime her husband, as a patent lawyer, became interested in various mechanical and electrical inventions that were beginning to appear. Telegraphy fascinated him in particular. He felt that the monopolistic Western Union Telegraph Company's rates were far too high and that this was detrimental to the economy. Hubbard contended that if the post office received and delivered telegrams, a private company could build the lines and transmit the messages more economically. He lobbied Congress for what became known as the Hubbard Bill. It proposed a private corporation charter to be known as the United States Postal Telegraph Company. As one of the incorporators, he would become a major figure in the nation's telegraph industry. It took up a great deal of his time in Washington. Consequently, the Hubbards decided not to open their Cambridge home, but rather to divide their time between Washington and New York.

Mrs. Hubbard continued to worry over Mabel's articulation. Like so many of the teachers of the deaf, Mary True had been impressed by Professor Bell's accomplishments. She decided to take Mabel to meet him. Mabel thought he sounded like a quack, but she agreed to go. She described their first encounter:

I both did and did not like him. He was so inter-

esting that I was forced to listen to him, but he himself I disliked. He dressed carelessly in a horribly shiny broadcloth, expensive but not fashionable, which made his jet-black hair look shiny. Altogether I did not think him exactly a gentleman.[2]

Mabel was not yet sixteen. She considered Professor Bell, who was in his late twenties, dreadfully old. "Why he must be over forty!" Yet as he talked with her, his flashing eyes and expressive mouth did much to dispel her prejudice. She admitted that he might be able to help her and was willing to enroll in his class. Mrs. Hubbard arranged for Mabel to spend that winter in Cambridge with her cousins, Mary and Carrie Blatchford. The months that followed provided Mabel with new and exciting experience. For the first time in her life an adult man found her fascinating. Bell was not in the least perturbed by her strange voice.

Miss Rogers and some other teachers claimed that the deaf could be taught to understand the speech of others by reading their lips; Bell was skeptical. Working with Mabel, who never took her eyes from his face, changed his mind. He delighted in talking with her; she was what he called a creative listener. He felt everything he had to say was of importance to her and was soon sharing his thoughts on many subjects, particularly the inventive ideas that were teeming in his brain. Letters to her mother were revealing:

Mr. Bell lost his train and insisted on taking me to the streetcar. We had a grand time running downhill through deep snow. I was nearly up to my knees in snow but it was so dry I didn't get wet and the run

22

kept me warmer than I generally am. I would have been almost sorry to get to the apothecary's but that I was quite out of breath; besides my waterproof and veil were flying about me and it was all I could do to hold on to them.[3]

Mr. Bell said today my voice was naturally sweet. Think of that! If I can only learn to use it properly, perhaps I will yet rival you in sweetness of voice. He continued pleased with me. He said today that he could make me do anything he chose. I enjoy my lessons very much and am glad you want me to stay. Everyone says it would be a pity to go away just as I am really trying to improve.[4]

In a postscript to another letter she added: "What do you think, I have been told I am beautiful!"[5]

Mabel was enjoying the winter in Cambridge, particularly the theater. She was a great admirer of Edwin Booth, the actor. Once she had the good fortune to be traveling on the same streetcar as the great man:

Our car arrived and we got in. Opposite sat two ladies and a gentleman. The gentleman was very handsome and grand looking with long black curly hair, beautiful black eyes and thin lips firmly closed betraying a spirit of determination. It was Edwin Booth himself! There could be no doubt of it. He looked just as he did in Hamlet, only not melancholy.[6]

But even so, Mabel longed for her family, especially since they were facing a financial crisis. Hubbard's campaign for the United States Postal Telegraph Company had so absorbed his time and energy that his business and professional interests suffered. He became indebted to his father-in-law and considered selling some of his Cambridge property, even their home. Mabel's journal voiced her concern:

Sometimes it seems so sad to go on living like this with no settled home; our family divided, part in New York, Papa in Washington and I living in Cambridge. It seems to me our "if" grows more frequent when we talk of having a home. Our house, that sweet home where we were born, still remains to us but a large placard distinctly announces that this estate is for sale; another says it is to let; another still that plants and flowers are for sale. It seems sometimes as if it were almost better to have sold it than to see it looking so lonely and uninhabitable. Mama talks of coming and opening the house for the summer but she won't do it unless Gramma comes too, so I am quite certain that such a pleasure is not in store for us.[7]

Mrs. Hubbard did reopen the house that summer, and in October 1874 Bell came for tea, played the piano and discussed his experiments with Hubbard enthusiastically. Bell became a frequent visitor to the Hubbard home, and because of their common interests in the deaf and telegraphy, the two men became friends. Eventually, with Mr. Thomas Sanders, the father of Bell's pupil George, they formed a partnership. Bell continued with his Boston University lectures, his special classes for teachers of the deaf and his private pupils, working on his inventions in his spare time.

4
The Engagement

BY THE AGE OF SIXTEEN, Mabel was becoming quite the young woman. Mrs. Hubbard described her first dance, which was held in their Cambridge home in 1874:

She was very disappointed that Edith and Annie Longfellow [daughters of the poet] couldn't come and wanted the dance put off. At 8:00 P.M. seven young ladies appeared, then the youth straggled in. Soon Mr. Bell arrived and our music commenced. When the company had all arrived, they were about twenty in number, Mabel received and introduced them with the greatest ease and self-possession and then Harcourt Amory led off in a waltz. He is a nice pleasant-looking young fellow and very friendly and polite to Mabel and one look at her face told how happy she was. I wish you could have seen her, so fresh, so full of enjoyment and so very pretty. She wore her peach silk and looked her loveliest.

She has just come into my room and I told her how pleased I was with her. She dropped her half-eaten apple and throwing her arms around my neck said, "Oh Mama, I am so glad, I would rather please you than anything else in the world." She confessed to some trepidation when the company began to arrive. She said that her lips trembled so that at first she could hardly speak but she didn't show it and I looked on amazed and delighted.[1]

By the spring of 1875, Bell had concluded a formal agreement with his backers, Sanders and Hubbard. Each agreed to contribute one-half of all expenses incurred in perfecting Bell's telegraphic inventions and in taking out and defending all related patents. Profits from these inventions were to be shared equally among the three of them.

Although Bell tried to carry on with his teaching, Hubbard pressed him to spend more and more time on his multiple telegraph. Before long he was spending most of his days and nights working on this invention to the detriment of his classes. Since he was not being paid for his time, he found himself seriously short of money.

Mabel continued her articulation lessons under Bell's assistant, Miss Locke. Bell was seldom present. However, he still visited the Hubbard home. The companionship of the four lively Hubbard daughters must have been a delightful change from his lonely life as an inventor. Grace and Berta, now aged fourteen and sixteen, mimicked Bell wickedly, impersonating his punctilious speech and formal manners. They too thought of him as being over forty. So when this pale, serious and impetuous man began falling in love with Mabel, the young sisters were the first to be aware of it and teased her unmercifully.

When Bell learned that Mabel would soon be leaving Cambridge to visit her cousin in Nantucket and that he might not see her for several months, he wrote in desperation to Mrs. Hubbard telling her of his love for Mabel. Concerned by how Mabel and her parents might feel about his intentions, he wrote confidentially to Mrs. Hubbard: "I promise beforehand to abide by your decision."[2]

26

Mabel was now seventeen, but in many ways she was young for her age, and deafness had made her terribly dependent on her family. The Hubbards decided that she was too young to be told of Bell's declaration and that she needed time to meet other young men before making any commitment. Mrs. Hubbard asked Bell to hide his feelings for a year.

In Nantucket Mabel's cousin, Mary Blatchford, explained the situation and suggested that Mabel might wish to make up her mind before returning home. In a whirl of emotion Mabel wrote to her mother:

I think I am old enough to have a right to know if he spoke about it to you and Papa. I know I am not much of a woman yet, but I feel very very much that this is to have...my whole future life in my hands.... Oh Mama, it came to me more and more that I am a woman such as I did not know before I was. I felt and feel so much of a child still.... Of course it cannot be, however clever and smart Mr. Bell may be; and however much honored I should be by being his wife, I never could love him or ever like him thoroughly....

Oh, it is such a grand thing to be a woman, a thinking, feeling and acting woman. But it is strange I don't feel at all as if I had won a man's love. Even if Mr. Bell does ask me, I shall not feel as if he did it through love.[3]

Mrs. Hubbard read part of Mabel's letter to Bell. In spite of its tone he was determined to go to Nantucket and talk with her. But before going, he wrote to Mrs. Hubbard:

The letter which you read to me yesterday was not the production of a girl—but of a true noble-

hearted woman—and she should be treated as such. I
shall show my respect for her by going to Nantucket
whether she will see me there or not.... I shall not ask
permission from you now...but shall merely go.[4]

At the Ocean House in Nantucket Bell passed a
sleepless night. Next day a violent rainstorm deluged the
island. He spent much of the day on a long letter to Mabel:

I have loved you with a passionate attachment
that you cannot understand, and that is to myself new
and incomprehensible. I wished [in Cambridge] to tell
you of my wish to make you my wife—if you would let
me try to win your love.

He went on to tell her of his promise to keep silent
and how distressed he was by her letter to her mother inti-
mating that she did not trust him. He reviewed what had
passed between her parents and himself and then
concluded:

It is for you to say whether you will see me or
not. You do not know—you cannot guess—how much
I love you.... I want you to know me better before you
dislike me.... I wish to amend my life for you.

When he called next day, Mabel hesitated to see
him. To Miss Blatchford's surprise, Bell readily departed.
The letter, he rightly sensed, would serve his purpose better than a face-to-face encounter.

Mabel acknowledged his letter:

Thank you very much for the honorable and generous way in which you treated me. Indeed you have
both my respect and esteem. I shall be glad to see you in
Cambridge and become better acquainted with you.

When Mabel returned from Nantucket, the Hub-

28

bards had Bell over for "a delightful and encouraging evening," as he reported in his journal. Meanwhile, he pushed his advantage with the Hubbards:

I feel myself still hampered by promises that I should not have made—I must be free to do whatever I think right and best—quite irrespective of your wishes—or of those of other people.

When I am in a position to offer a home, I wish to marry her—whether it is in two years or two months!... If you do not like my conduct in the matter, you can deny me the house—and I can wait.

From Mrs. Hubbard came this satisfactory reply:

I give you back your promise, entirely, unreservedly. I believe your love for my Mabel to be unselfish and noble. I trust you perfectly. If you can win her love, I shall feel happy in my darling's happiness.

And she invited him to call. The next day, August 26, 1875, he described as "the happiest day of my life." That evening in the greenhouse he and Mabel at last talked freely and alone. She did not love him, she said, but she did not dislike him. It was enough. In the journal he had opened to chronicle his courtship, he wrote triumphantly: "Shall not record any more here. I feel that I have at last got to the end of all my troubles—and whatever happens I may now safely write: FINIS!"

Bell went home to Brantford for the rest of the summer to recuperate from the strain of both his work and his emotional life. He remained there until October, bringing back with him the beginning of an American patent specification for his telephone. He resolved that as soon as he finished drafting the patent specifications, he would suspend

29

all work on his inventions and concentrate on teaching. He would organize a teacher-training course to include visible speech so that institutions for the deaf should have a supply of fully trained teachers. He would also canvass for private pupils, which would help to provide him with an adequate living. Hubbard objected strenuously to his plan:

I have been sorry to see how little interest you seem to take in telegraph matters. Your frenzy for teaching confirms the tendency of your mind to undertake every new thing that interests you and accomplish nothing of any value to anyone. Your whole course since your return has been a great disappointment to me and a sore trial.

Somehow Bell managed for a time not only to mollify Gardiner Hubbard but also to court Mabel. He wrote her: "You must not think that my visits to Cambridge are hindering me in my work, they are having just the opposite effect."[5] Nevertheless, harried and hard-pressed, he wrote her an emotional plea not to encourage him out of pity but to let him know at once if she could not sincerely return his love. Then he had to soothe away her hurt at being suspected of thoughtless trifling.

Hubbard brought matters to a climax just before Thanksgiving. He demanded that Bell choose between teaching and visible speech on the one hand and telegraphy and Mabel on the other, offering to furnish Bell's living expenses in the latter case. Bell exploded. Precisely because he loved Hubbard's daughter and prized Hubbard's respect, he would not accept any special favours. The existing agreement was perfectly fair. As for visible speech, it had been the life work of Alec's father; to further it would be Alec's life work, whatever Hubbard or anyone else thought of it. He had become a teacher because he was needed and he was still needed. He had the power to free deaf and stammering children from what amounted to life imprisonment for no crime. He would not withhold it, at least not until he had qualified others to take his place. Fortunately for his marriage hopes, his work lecturing at the School of Oratory at Boston University was at last bringing him a respectable income—currently at the rate of four or five thousand dollars a year. He was sorry if Hubbard did not like his profession, but he did not propose changing it. And if Mabel loved him, she would marry him anyway.

Some weeks later he wrote in a more temperate vein, not shifting his views, but apologizing for any apparent disrespect and gratefully acknowledging Hubbard's "sincere interest in my welfare independently of any pecuniary interest...in my inventions. Please bear with me for a little longer."

Perhaps as much as his firm stand and conciliatory letter, Mabel's reaction helped bring her father around. She resented her father presuming to make him choose between her hand and his profession. Her mother, feeling his love to be unselfish and true, urged her daughter either to give him up or to consent to become engaged at once. When he came to call on Mabel's eighteenth birthday, November 25, 1875, also Thanksgiving Day, she told him that she loved him better than anyone but her mother, and if that satisfied him, she was willing to become engaged to him.

Mabel took him by surprise at what seemed to him a time of utter despair. Conscience compelled him to re-

31

mind her again of her youth and how little she had seen of other men. But she told him that she knew she would never find anyone else to love as well. The commitment was made, and for the rest of their lives Thanksgiving Day would hold a special significance.

After Mabel's earlier insistence that she "never could love him or ever like him thoroughly," one might well wonder what had transpired during the preceding twelve months to make her change her mind. At the time of Bell's first overtures she undoubtedly regarded him in the light of mentor rather than suitor. To this was added their differences in age, Mabel still considering herself a girl, while Bell, her mature and learned teacher, was so obviously an adult. A readjustment of her perceptions of him needed time.

And finally, there was the gnawing matter of money, always an important consideration during courtship. Mabel was aware of Bell's precarious financial position in the same way that she realized her father was no longer as rich as he had been. She knew her father had been supporting Bell's experiments out of his own pocket, and this too would have caused her to reflect on his ability to support her in a satisfactory manner after they were married. It is likely that Bell's firm devotion and strength of mind won her over in the end.

5
Courtship

ONCE ENGAGED, Mabel could call Mr. Bell "Alec," and her comments to him became frank and wholehearted. On the day following their engagement she wrote:

I have been feeling so troubled and frightened at what I did yesterday. I do not regret it and never will but it is such a solemn thing. I feel the responsibility very much. It has made me very nervous and almost doubting if I have enough love to give, but I trust in your love and feel strong and sure in it.[1]

And later:

I love you very much and with the exception of a few little things which are mostly on the outside, I would not have you changed from what you are now. I warned you before we were engaged that although I might love you very much, I could not do so in the passionate, hot way that you do and you took me in spite of it. I love you all I can and my powers of loving seem to increase daily. You must be satisfied with this. I would give you more if I could but I cannot help my nature.[2]

Shortly afterwards Mabel tried to correct some of the "little things which are mostly on the outside." When Alec went to visit her grandparents in New York for the first time, she wrote urging him to keep himself neat and tidy, otherwise she would be mortified. She need not have worried, however, for Mr. McCurdy was very impressed by Bell and pleased that Mabel had become engaged to him. He realized, perhaps more fully than her parents, that with her handicap she might never have an opportunity to marry. In spite of her intelligence and charm, few young men would wish to be saddled with a deaf wife. He thought Mabel extremely fortunate to have become engaged to a man with such an understanding of the problems of the deaf. Bell considered her deafness not so much a handicap as an added challenge to their love. Moreover, Mr. McCurdy approved of Mr. Bell's age and had no objections to his teaching profession.

Alec's father wrote to Mabel, describing his son as being hotheaded but warmhearted, sentimental, dreamy and obstinate but sincere and unselfish. He was ambitious to a fault, apt to let enthusiasm run away with judgment, and there was no doubt procrastination was one of his besetting sins. Mrs. Hubbard declared that he had more sides than a prism, and she was always interested to know what side he would show next.

Bell's lack of financial resources coupled with Hubbard's insistence that he devote all his energies to perfecting his multiple telegraph and telephone put a strain on their courtship. If Mabel had not been so interested, she might have felt neglected as Alec and her father spent hours discussing his inventions. Only when they were out walking or driving together did she really have him to herself. If it happened to be a dark night, communication between them was difficult. Only under the street lights could Mabel see to read her lover's lips. A casual passerby must have been surprised to see an exquisitely dressed young lady and her companion dashing from one street lamp to the next. If they were driving together on a dark night it was not unusual for them to take candles along. Every so often they would stop the horse, light a candle and carry on their conversation.

Throughout 1876 Bell was torn between the pressure put upon him by Hubbard to complete his specifications for the telephone and his desire to carry on his training of teachers for the deaf. He explained his predicament to Mabel:

I want to get enough [money] to take off the hardship of life and leave me free to follow out the ideas that interest me most. One thing I become more sure of every day—that my interest in the deaf is to be a lifelong thing with me. I see so much to be done—and so few to do it—so few qualified to do it. I shall never leave this work and you must settle down to the conviction that whatever success I may meet with in life—pecuniary or otherwise—your husband will be known as a teacher of the deaf.[3]

Unlike Hubbard, Bell's father felt that his son was devoting far too much time and energy to his experiments in telegraphy, and he urged him to sell his inventions to his backers, Hubbard and Sanders. He had no doubt that teaching the deaf was his son's true vocation. However, Mabel felt quite differently; she was much more interested in the scientific aspect of his career:

You don't know how much my heart is in your work and how anxious I am that you should succeed. I want so much that you should take your proper place among scientific men. I don't think you care very much about it, but for my sake and for the sake of oth-

35

ers who might depend on you, you ought to. That re-mark looks so selfish I am inclined to tear up this whole letter but I have no time for another note before the closing of the mails and besides what is for me is for you also.[4]

You know what I think of the telephone, but you do not know what I think of Visible Speech. This has been the one subject that we have both avoided. You do not know how much this has troubled me at times. I feel that if there is anything on which two persons do not agree, it must gradually grow to be a wall between them. There must be no such thing between us two and there will not be if we speak openly of it.

What I think of Visible Speech now is that it will be of greatest value to learners, deaf or hearing, but I think it will be a long time before it will come into general use. There may be money in it but you are not the one to get that money because you love your work and cannot bear to ask pay for that labor of love. I think of the two you are more likely to make something out of the telephone and if you do, you will be better able to carry out your work [for the deaf]. So for that reason I think it would be better if you made Visible Speech secondary to the telephone.... All I want you to do is to work away at electricity steadily at present, to try the lines between Brantford and Paris and do your utmost to induce someone to take up your foreign patents so as to allow you to go on working.[5]

Over the years people have suggested that Bell's invention of the telephone was the result of his endeavor to provide hearing for Mabel. Although his early experiments were carried out when she was studying articulation under his direction, the first experiments to devise an apparatus that might help deaf children—from which the telephone evolved—were initiated by his earlier work at the Horace Mann School. However, there is no doubt that their love affair did profoundly influence the development of the telephone. Mr. and Mrs. Hubbard and Mabel were all very enthusiastic and saw great possibilities in his experiments.

When Hubbard accepted responsibility for organizing an educational exhibit at the Centennial Exhibition held in Philadelphia in 1876, he invited Bell to send a display on visible speech. Mabel and her mother felt that this would be a wonderful opportunity for Alec to display his telephone. When they suggested it to him, he was shy about the idea, realizing that in order to demonstrate the telephone successfully it would require much more work. At the time he was preoccupied with preparing his teachers of the deaf for their final exams. Mabel kept urging Alec to make the necessary improvements, but by the time he did it was too late to have it assigned a place in the electrical section. Instead it was sandwiched in with the visible speech charts in an obscure corner of the educational exhibit.

A telegram arrived from Hubbard stating that the exhibition judges were expected to reach Bell's exhibit on Sunday, June 25, and that he must be there to demonstrate. Mabel and her mother were at their wit's end, knowing that Alec's final examinations for his speech classes were to be held during that last week of June. It took all of Mrs. Hubbard's tact as well as Mabel's tears to get him on the train for Philadelphia. That evening he wrote Mabel:

I must confess I don't see what good I can accomplish in Philadelphia unless I stay for a long time and as far as telegraphy is concerned, I shall be far happier and more honored if I can send out a band of competent teachers of the deaf and dumb who will accomplish a good work—than I should be to receive all the telegraphic honors in the world.[6]

Mabel promptly replied: "If you get a medal, you must give it to me for it was I who sent you after it. Won't I be gorgeous with the immense thing hanging around my neck."[7] She had been under great strain getting Alec off to Philadelphia:

How shall I tell you how happy and glad I have been that you are in Philadelphia with all the distinguished scientists who will understand and appreciate you and your discoveries. I have been so unhappy and worried about the thing for so long. I can hardly breathe freely yet but the more I think of it, the more relieved I am. It was very hard to send you off so unwillingly but I am sure it was for the best and you will be glad of it by and by. Don't get discouraged now. If you persevere, success must come. Anyway it will be a great help to you to be connected with scientific men. I have been thinking of you every spare moment. How I miss you![8]

That particular Sunday was one of the hottest of the year. The judging committee, accompanied by Dom Pedro, the emperor of Brazil, moved slowly from one exhibit to the next. They were hot and tired and anxious to return to their hotels. Bell's heart sank as they approached and he heard them announce that the exhibit just before his would be the last for that day. As the judges turned to leave, they stood aside to allow the emperor to precede them. In that moment Dom Pedro recognized Bell, whom he had met in Boston while making a study of American methods of education, and immediately came over to chat with him. When he learned how disappointed Bell felt that the judges would not be looking at his invention that day, Dom Pedro insisted the judges wait and see the telephone being demonstrated. Bell's telephone received the highest award as the most interesting exhibit. Mabel's efforts had finally brought him recognition as an inventor.

During their eighteen-month engagement Mabel and Alec were frequently separated, particularly in the summer when Alec visited his parents in Brantford, Ontario. During such times they wrote long letters to each other, not only sharing the events of each day and making plans for their future, but also exchanging ideas on a wide variety of subjects. Mabel wrote:

Mama and I had a long talk this afternoon about you and our plans. Mama says that you are a man of brilliant talents and you must make yours a useful life for the benefit of those around you and the world at large. They will procure you fame and money if you work steadily and concentrate all your thought and energy on the things at hand. But your mind is so fragile—it is always drawn off to every new idea that comes up. You like to fly around like a butterfly, sipping honey more or less from flower to flower. But this is not the way to accomplish anything. You will never do anything of value that way. She thinks it is well that

you have to support a wife. If I came to you rich, you might think you had nothing to do but please yourself. Having to support me will give you a purpose and will help to give you that stability and perseverance that you lack.[9]

Mabel was greatly troubled when she learned that her father had written Alec a sharp letter accusing him of procrastination in preparing his telephone specifications:

This slowness and procrastination...I think is your great fault and mine also, and I don't know what we are going to do if this goes on. I am trying so hard to conquer this in myself. Cannot we join and each try to conquer it in ourselves? They say two can do much more than one. If I were only smart like Berta, this in you might not matter so much; or if you were like Papa who pushes through everything regardless of whether he is sick or well. But since we both have it, I fear that one effort alone can do little. Let us resolve that when there is a thing to be done, we will do it quickly and let no other thing interfere with it. I know I shall fail over and over again. Still let us try and surely if we put our whole will to it and ask God's help, we shall in the end succeed. Then our friends will not be disappointed in us and will not be afraid to trust us.[10]

Another subject they discussed was women's rights. Bell was a staunch supporter of women's rights. She replied:

Thank you for telling me all you think about Women's Rights. I was only afraid you would give me credit for more earnestness on this subject than I feel. My interest is of very recent date and all I know about it has been gathered from what Miss True's sister, and lately you, have said about it. So far as I am concerned the laws, both civil and society, may stay as they please. I am not at all envious of men but I do not think it is just or right that women must depend as much as they do on men's sense of justice or love which is all that restrain them from using the great power they possess. How may we be sure interest will not triumph over the one, or other feelings take the place of the latter?

A man can put his wife in prison for keeping her own money from him and use that money in a lawsuit against her. The idea "of marriage as a union and complete identity of two beings, so perfect a union that what belongs to the one belongs to the other," is indeed beautiful, but before the law does the man really do as he says in the Episcopal marriage service "with all my worldly goods I thee endow"? I only know that the promise becomes null and void at his death when only one-third of his estate goes to his widow if he has no children.

I do not sympathize with the "extremity" any more than you do, and would not have the public sentiment that forbids women to appear in public life, or to assume duties hitherto belonging exclusively to men, outraged if it could be helped. But there are so many more women than men, that not all can have home duties to occupy them and they are obliged to seek other work or live a useless life.

Not all can be dressmakers or governesses, they must go forth and be doctors, artists, professors or preachers as their talent inclines them. They do not interfere with you men for you have more than enough work and in some respects they may be better fitted for the work than you. They are more tender and delicate of touch and have greater sensitivity and keener perception than you and perhaps this may make up for lack of strength.[11]

Religion was another matter discussed at some length. The subject first came up while Mabel was visiting Hartford in the home of Mr. and Mrs. Barnard. Barnard was a Protestant married to the daughter of a Catholic refugee, and all the children were Catholic:

I am so glad we are of the same religion. I cannot understand how there can be perfect confidence and oneness between two people holding such different opinions on such deep and important matters. There must be always something about which they cannot speak. I cannot see how a husband and wife can go on like that—loving each other so much. I think if you were Catholic, I should try to be one too. Anything rather than separation.[12]

Bell replied to this letter by stating his religious beliefs:

I cannot believe in the inherent wickedness of man. The world seems very beautiful to me, and there seems to me to be more good about mankind per se than bad.... Concerning Death and Immortality, Salvation, Faith and all the other points of theoretical religion, I know absolutely nothing and can frame no beliefs whatever. Men should be judged not by their religious beliefs but by their lives.[13]

He went on to explain that he asked that much and no more for himself. He was glad for Mabel's sake that she had religious faith, and he did not want his agnosticism to weaken it. Neither did he want her to take him for what he was not. In response to her further questions he wrote:

I hope for life after death but cannot accept it as certain. My religious beliefs, or rather non-beliefs, are a source of grief to my poor mother who prays constantly for her misguided son.[14]

Mabel replied to this letter:

As for your not having time to speak to me about these things before our engagement...I knew you were not orthodox in most of your beliefs, in fact I went further and believed you were an atheist, so you see, I have not to learn that you were worse but better than I thought. Yes, it is a privilege to live but I think it would be perfectly dreadful if we have no hope after this life. This life is so short and so full of sorrow that it would be miserable to live on after a loved one had gone and to feel that the parting was final; that there would be no meeting again. It is so glorious and comforting to know there is something after this—that everything does not end with this world.[15]

An interesting and unusual experience was in store for Mabel during November and December of 1876: the opportunity to travel by train across the continent at a time when the West was just beginning to develop. The president of the United States appointed her father chairman of a special commission to investigate the problem of transporting the mails by railway. The commissioners and

43

some members of their families traveled in luxury by private railway cars.

Mabel wrote almost daily letters to Alec in which she described the passing scenery:

I am disappointed in Chicago, the rebuilt part of the city already looks as old as a European town, such damage has the smoke and soot done [from the great fire]. The streets are worse than those around Faneuil Hall, Boston. The sidewalks are so queer, mostly three feet above the driveway, and are ascended by dilapidated wooden steps little distances apart. The whole city, so far as I have seen, has such a disagreeable unfinished look, the streets where the fine houses are, are grass grown along the sides and the wooden sidewalks here and there look shiftless. But the few fine buildings are really fine and when Chicago gets settled down, the streets kept clean and the rubbish cleared away, it will look like a fine old world city.[16]

The prairies appeared from her train window:

Shanties grow fewer and further between them and more miserable and the broad level Prairies are divided by no fences except now and then a snow-fence or a little stockade protecting the small dominion of some squatter. Some of the houses are made of earth dried in the sun and the cattle sheds are thatched with straw—all of the poorest and most primitive description. We passed a little caravan of emigrants and I thought what a graphic picture they would make; the quaint white-covered emigrant wagons huddled closely together after their night's rest, the dreary yellow Prairie stretching way to the barren bluffs in the dis-

tance and no other human habitation in sight.[17]

They broke their journey at Salt Lake City, so Mabel had ample opportunity to see it at close range:

Opposite is the fine unfinished residence of Brigham Young's eighteenth and favorite wife Amelia, of gray granite with lilac facings, three storeys and a tower, and all modern improvements.... All his wives seem to have houses of their own but none of them half as fine or big as Amelia's. He has ninety-four children! I wouldn't be a Mormon wife for the world or share you with any living woman—at least it would be horrible to have to.[18]

Her fascinating experiences did not overshadow her concern for Alec and his work. Writing from Denver, Colorado, she said:

I am thankful that the specification is on its way at last and I hope you may be able to procure patents without incurring any debts. I have a great dread of them—having an idea of how they weigh you down when you are unable to pay them, but I am extremely sorry you think of giving up your Christmas visit home. Your mother will be so disappointed and will not think much better of the telephone as its cause, or us for encouraging it. I do wish I could help you, but of course, like every other foolishly honorable man, you prefer to borrow from everyone else rather than from the one who is most interested in your success or failure, so I shall not offer.[19]

When Mabel returned home, she and Alec were anxious to be married. Mrs. Hubbard continued to favor Bell's suit for her daughter's hand, but was concerned about his financial prospects. Her concern prompted Bell to offer his telephone patents to the Western Union Telegraph Company for $100,000, but the offer was refused on the grounds that the company had no use for an electrical toy. It looked as if the marriage would have to be postponed indefinitely.

Fortunately, in June 1877, Bell came to an agreement with William H. Reynolds, a Providence, Rhode Island, broker, to purchase a portion of the English patent for $5,000. It was arranged that Bell should go to England with Reynolds and assist in obtaining capital for the establishment of an English telephone company.

Alec and Mabel were to be married before he left, so Mabel and her mother busied themselves preparing the trousseau. Unfortunately, Mrs. Hubbard's mother, Mrs. McCurdy, died in December 1876, and the whole family went into mourning. For a time Alec thought Mabel might appear on her wedding day dressed in black. Her wedding dress turned out to be a simple white gown. Nevertheless, family tradition overrode Alec's wishes with respect to her trousseau:

Alec dear, do you mind so much my wearing black after the wedding? I spoke to Mama about it and she told me if you didn't feel very strongly about it, she wanted me to retain my black. You English, for you are English, wear mourning for a very short time. Here it is the custom to put it on seldom but when you do, you wear it for a long time. She said she felt very strongly about it; if I put on colors, it would seem as if you had taken me away from my family, that I cared no longer about them and their sorrow. I will not wear

my dull black dress that you think so somber and I never had any intentions to wear crepe. All I want to wear is pretty black and white silk and lavender in the evening, that will not be mourning and will be bright and pretty and yet not so much that I and my family will feel separated.[20]

Again, she writes of her wedding plans:

I have taken you at your word and have been looking for things for my trousseau, very quiet and modest, but I think they will be very pretty. Such an amount of needlework for us all. I, for one, enjoy the prospect of marriage but how I shall like the realization is another thing. I proposed eloping as the simplest and less troublesome way of getting married. But oh, Mama forbids my proposing such a thing to you for fear you might decide it is the proper thing to do.[21]

The marriage took place on July 11, 1877, at the Hubbard home on Brattle Street, Cambridge, in a room fragrant with the scent of Madonna lilies that the gardener had saved for the occasion.

Alec's present to her was an exquisite cross of eleven round pearls. And soon after their marriage he turned over to his bride all but ten of his 1,507 shares in the Bell Telephone Company.[22] Bell's explanation was that he could not promise "with all my worldly goods I thee endow" without actually doing so. In later years his daughter would laugh when he told this story and say, "That is all very well, but you got rid of having to attend to any family financial matters." It was quite true; Mabel Bell relieved her husband of all such responsibilities.

6
First Year of Marriage

LIKE ANY BRIDE, Mabel found the first months of marriage a period of adjustment. Except for holidays and the one winter in Vienna, she had never been away from her family. Boston was full of Hubbard relations, and when in New York she was surrounded by her McCurdy aunts and uncles and her grandfather, to whom she was very special. Now she was embarking on an entirely different kind of life in England with her new husband.

They honeymooned at Niagara Falls, then went on to Brantford to visit Alec's family. She had already met his father in Boston, but this was her first meeting with Mrs. Bell. Alec's uncle, David Bell, met them at the station and drove them the four miles out of town to Tutelo Heights where Alec's mother was waiting. Before Mabel had time to speak, Mrs. Bell broke an oatcake over her head. Alec explained the old Scottish custom and that it was considered very unlucky if a bride entered her husband's home without first undergoing this ritual. The oatcake was a symbol that she would never go hungry. Writing to her mother describing this startling encounter, she observed:

Mrs. Bell is just as nice and kind as she can be, so bright and quick. I do think she enjoys this life in Canada though I understand why Alec feels so badly about it [her having had to give up her life in London

Mabel Hubbard Bell as a child; her teacher, Mary True; below, Mabel as a teen; left, Mabel's father, Gardiner Hubbard, and her mother, Gertrude McCurdy Hubbard.

Mabel and Alexander, with their daughters Elsie May and
Marian (Daisy), the year they first visited Baddeck, 1885.

Marian and Elsie May; below, four generations:
Gertrude Hubbard, Melville Grosvenor, his mother,
Elsie May Grosvenor and Mabel Bell

Mabel's parents
Gertrude and Gardiner Hubbard about 1890

Left: Mabel measuring kite pull. Below: Mabel at Beinn Bhreagh.

Mabel in a diving suit; the Bells visit Sable Island; with a tetrahedral kite frame; below: the Bells with their daughters, grand-children, and sons-in-law Gilbert Grosvenor (left) and David Fairchild.

Aerial Experiment Association: Glenn Curtiss, Casey Baldwin, Alexander Graham Bell, Tom Selfridge, and Douglas McCurdy. Below, Bell on the wharf intently watching the HD4 travel across the Bras d'Or Lake–Mabel is at the wheel.

Above: Mabel in her study, 1922. Below: The funeral of
Alexander Graham Bell. A few months later, Mabel's ashes were
placed in the same grave.

for the sake of Alec's health]. It is so funny to see him here. He is so different from them all and actually seems a great dandy.[1]

Alec's parents entertained for them the following evening with a party of their friends and neighbors, including the local member of Parliament, farmers, lawyers and even the Indian chief of the Six Nations, Chief Johnson. Alec demonstrated his telephone for the benefit of the guests, and Chief Johnson talked into it in the Mohawk language. To the refined bride from Cambridge it was the most democratic gathering she had ever attended.

They returned to Boston, and soon after, on August 4, 1877, seven years after his arrival in America, Alexander Graham Bell and his bride sailed from New York to England on the S.S. *Anchoria.* In spite of bad weather, the voyage was pleasant. They sat at the captain's table, and the other guests, responding to Mabel's look of radiance, were so attentive that Alec complained he never had a chance to speak to her.

In the evenings Alec played the piano for the passengers while Mabel danced. Although she could not hear the music, and had had to learn to balance by sight since the scarlet fever had destroyed her inner ear passages, she could feel the piano's vibrations. She was never seasick, nor did she become dizzy—no matter how often she was whirled around the dance floor. Alec demonstrated the telephone, which afforded everyone a great deal of pleasure and amusement. They docked at Greenock and shortly after their arrival in Glasgow she wrote her mother:

Here we are safely on shore again in Alec's beloved "ain country." The poor fellow is perfectly wild

49

over it and is so anxious to have me like everything because it is Scotch and especially anything that is from Edinburgh, it is really pathetic. He almost went down on his knees to beg me to like Edinburgh breakfast rolls.[2]

They spent a few days in Glasgow. The first day provided some indication of what her days in England would be like. Alec set out after breakfast to visit his boyhood friends, the Henderson brothers. When he returned to the hotel five or six hours later he was accompanied by the postmaster and superintendent of telegraphs, with whom he'd spent the greater part of the day carrying out experiments. Mabel shared Alec's pleasure when he told her that before the experiments the gentlemen had been polite, but afterwards treated him almost with veneration. One gentleman said that after this he would believe anything he heard from America, no matter how wonderful or incredible it might seem. The postmaster asked Alec, through the telephone, if he would mind exhibiting it again before the chief citizens of Glasgow and the press.

While they were being entertained by Professor Thomson in Glasgow, a telegram arrived from his brother, Sir William Thomson, later to become Lord Kelvin. Sir William had been one of the judges at the Centennial Exhibition in Philadelphia, and Bell had given him a set of telephones to take back to England. He invited the Bells to join him in Plymouth where he was attending a meeting of the British Association for the Advancement of Science. William Henry Preece, a British electrical expert, had given a paper on the telephone that had caused a sensation, and the members of the association were anxious to meet the inventor. Bell was confident he could impress this august

50

body of scientists, but Mabel had a moment of self-doubt:

Tomorrow we will be in Plymouth, probably at the center of attention, and I am so frightened to think how ill I can act my part as Graham Bell's wife. This is the only name Alec is known by up here. Oh, I wish I were safe at home, I'd give up all hope of ever being Lady Bell and all the glories of being the wife of a successful inventor, everything but just being Alec's wife, to come home to quiet humbleness. Not that I am not enjoying myself nor that everyone is not very kind.

Who do you think asked to be introduced to Alec today but Sir Willoughby Jones. He brought Alec up to Lady Jones and they seemed very proud to meet him. They invited us to dine with them tomorrow but we had to decline because we are dining with Sir William and Lady Thomson on their yacht. Lady Jones will call on me tomorrow morning. Alec is really the chief person here. Everybody seeks to do him honor. He has been introduced to all the great people, Lord this and Sir that, and all are anxious and eager to speak with him.[3]

As a result of Sir William Thomson's praise and the excellent press reports, Bell was showered with so many invitations to speak that he was unable to accept them all. During the first four months after his arrival he gave at least ten telephone lectures in England and Scotland, sponsored mainly by scientific and technical societies, but to which the general public was also invited. On at least two occasions over two thousand people turned up.

One of his first lectures was in Aberdeen. On their way to fulfill this engagement they stopped over in Edinburgh and Alec took Mabel to Charlotte Square to show her his old family home. He was delighted to see that the opaque windows were still in the house next door and explained to Mabel how he and his young brother used to stand at the nursery window in their night clothes making faces at the young ladies attending school in that house. Finally, in desperation, the head mistress put in the opaque glass to conceal the proper young ladies from the naughty boys.

Although only late September, Mabel found Aberdeen very cold and rather dreaded going farther north to Banff and Elgin and the little seaside village of Covesea. But Alec had set his heart on their having a second honeymoon in that area of Scotland that held such happy memories of his early teaching days. He suggested they stay in a humble fisherman's cottage and rough it. They would lay in a stock of preserved meats and other supplies, but would live chiefly by catching and cooking their own fish. Mabel, a little concerned over this prospect, realized that they had seldom seen a fish being cooked, and neither of them had ever attempted doing it themselves. Alec thought it a simple operation, but Mabel was under the impression that the fish had to be opened and a part of its inside taken out. She described the experience to her mother:

We engaged the funniest little room you ever saw. The ceiling is so low that Alec's tip-top curl almost brushes against it. The room has tiny diamond-paned windows. The green painted walls are covered with countless little pictures from newspapers, giving the room a most fantastic air.

We are to provide our own food and fuel, and how I am to manage cooking on a little grate I don't know and Alec is so aggravating in his sublime ignor-

ance of any difficulty in the matter. A pleasant-faced woman offered to do anything for us and Alec actually told her he thought all we would need was hot water. However, Mrs. Cameron supplied us with some nice fresh milk and eggs. We have bought a little portable tea kettle and boiled our tea and eggs in it but alas two trials were sufficient to break Alec's courage and now to my great joy Mrs. Cameron boils our eggs, tea and potatoes for us. The only thing Alec won't trust her to do is to prepare his beloved smoked herrings. He did them himself at first but the fire gave him a headache so he allowed me to do it.

Alec insisted that a loaf of bread, half a pound of sugar and a pound of butter was quite enough to last us the week. I am rather triumphant for this morning Mrs. Cameron's lassie had to walk three miles to Lossiemouth for some more. Alec meant to have gone this morning at six, but of course when Mrs. Cameron called him, he turned over on his side and went to sleep again. My sugar ought to have lasted longer but that husband of mine wasted six or seven good lumps trying experiments to find out if it was the sugar itself or the air in the sugar that exploded when melted in a cup of hot tea or water causing little fountains of water at the surface which you can see only by holding the cup to the light. He decided it was the air.

Ever since Saturday we have been out on the rocks each day. Saturday we carried provisions but quarreled so over them and found them so heavy that yesterday we left all behind.

What a man my husband is! I am perfectly bewildered at the number and size of the ideas with which his head is crammed. Flying machines to which telephones and torpedoes are to be attached occupy the first place just now from the observation of seagulls and the practicability of attaching telephones to wire fences. His mind is full of both these things. Every now and then he comes back with another flying machine which has quite changed its shape within a quarter of an hour.

Then he goes climbing about the rocks forming theories of the origin of cliffs and caves, which last problem he has solved to his satisfaction. Then he comes home and watches the sugar bubbles. Starts out next morning after rabbits, but I have no doubt he pays more attention to the seagulls but seems as anxious to prove himself a good shot as any school boy.[4]

Their last day at Covesea was the climax to a gorgeous week. Mabel took her sketchbook and sat on the rocks while Alec composed verses, which he wrote in the sand. The verses claimed that he wrote "with a saddened heart and trembling hand," but Mabel reported that he looked anything but sad, dancing about wildly in his bare feet:

I tried to sketch him as he stood still for a few moments thinking of a rhyme, his feet bare and rather far apart, his hands outstretched. The sketch was a failure so far at least as any likeness was concerned, but I wish you could have seen him. He was so wild and full of fun though rather ashamed that the inventor of the telephone should go wading, but I persuaded him that he should not be a slave to his own position.[5]

About this time Mabel's suspicion that she might be

pregnant was confirmed, and like most young women in that condition, she was torn between consternation and delight. Alec marked the occasion by giving her a tiny pair of baby's socks. She was greatly amused when someone saw them with the socks and asked how old the baby was.

On their way to London they stopped again in Glasgow where Alec gave a lecture for which he was paid fifteen pounds, ten shillings. The practical Mabel commented: "I am glad to have it settled beforehand, for the Aberdeen people have not said a word about payment now their lecture is over."[6] On arrival in London the Bells took rooms in a fashionable West End private hotel on Jermyn Street. Bell considered it important for the new company he was helping to promote that "they should make as good a show as possible."[7]

These were busy days for him. In addition to his own experimental work, he traveled all over Great Britain superintending the preliminary tests that were to interest English capital in the telephone, even finding time to deliver a number of lectures on the education of the deaf. Freed from the uncertainties and strain of his Boston years, he expanded under the acclaim the English scientific world afforded him and became very happy in his personal life. He regarded these few months in Britain as the most satisfactory—professionally as well as personally—of any period in his life. This sense of satisfaction was reflected in his growing girth, and by Christmas he had put on a great deal of weight, as Mabel noted in a letter to her mother:

To think that not only a whole week but Christmas day has passed without my writing you. I am sorry, I thought I would have all day yesterday to write

and it is not my fault or Alec's but his two hundred and one pounds that kept me from doing so.

Why, Mama dear, he had his wedding trousers made larger some time ago and who would have thought that they would so soon be tight again in that they'd burst. It happened the day before yesterday and I forgot all about it until I was going to write. My afternoon went in darning that terrible tear that grew larger the more I stitched.... Was it not horrible when later on in the evening when Alec stooped to put out some Christmas candles that had caught fire, they should burst again in the very same place and all my hours of work lost.[8]

Life was not all joy for Mabel during this first year of marriage. The damp climate and heavy gray skies of London were a poor substitute for the brilliance of a New England autumn, but most of all she missed her family. She tried to keep herself busy by writing her husband's letters and translating German scientific articles for him, but hotel life wearied her:

You have no idea how tired and homesick I have been living here with nothing to do to induce me to try and keep our rooms looking nice. It is no use, Alec has no room for his papers and they are always scattered about the room on chairs and on the floor and every day the piles increase in spite of my daily sorting. The only writing table is small and will not hold half the things Alec is always wanting so he uses the dining table and at mealtime the waiter sweeps the papers all together and piles them up here and there creating greater confusion and putting Alec out and destroying

my work of hours of arranging. Then Miss Brooks, the proprietress, does not like the telephone. Alec wants a house where he can run wires from top to bottom to rooms out of earshot and where he would be free to do as he likes. Of course, in a place like this the owner would always be interfering and Alec's nightly labors make trouble. People don't like to have men striding up and down over their heads all night long as Alec does. Alec is quite as anxious, if not more so, than I am, to have a home of our own.[9]

In November they took a furnished house at 57 West Cromwell Road, South Kensington, and were much happier. They had a dining room and study on the ground floor, a parlor and bedroom on the second, several small bedrooms on the third and fourth, and a lovely large garden at the rear. They were fortunate in obtaining the services of Mary Home. She had been housekeeper for many years with Alec's grandfather until the time of his death. A friend recommended a suitable parlor maid, but they remained in need of a secretary:

Alec says he is glad he took this house for I am so much better and happier than in those rooms. I hate the thought of them. Alec himself is happy in this land of dreams or will be as soon as his secretary comes to take the correspondence that weighs him down. He has failed to get a satisfactory one yet.[10]

Apparently Mabel's newly acquired domestic responsibilities did not leave her time to continue acting as his secretary, for at this period the letters to her mother are full of requests for recipes:

I should like your recipe for whips and floating

island as I do not like the English puddings. How do you make fish balls? What can I do with the remains of cold chicken? Could I serve it up with curry the next day? I don't want to waste anything.[11]

Although Mabel was much happier in a home of their own, she still suffered from loneliness. Alec didn't want her to go out alone as she had difficulty making herself understood in the London shops. Mary Home accompanied her to market, but Mabel longed for the company of her mother or sisters. Alec hated to leave a shop without buying something, whether it was what they wanted or not. When she remonstrated with him he would get impatient and she would end up in tears.

A recurring problem throughout her entire marriage was trying to get her husband up in the morning. At Jermyn Street he got into the habit of breakfasting at eleven, two hours later than Mabel. He complained of sleepless nights and bad headaches so she didn't have the heart to pull him out of bed, in fact, she couldn't. However, at West Cromwell Road she was more successful and they breakfasted together at eight-thirty:

He often feels cross and headachy when I wake him and begs hard to stay in bed but if I am firm, after breakfast, the headache has quite disappeared and he is bright and thankful he has been awakened. Yet it is hard work and tears are spent over it sometimes.[12]

Recognition continued to come to Bell. There was a special meeting of the Society of Telegraph Engineers in London to welcome him. On Boxing Day a telephone demonstration at the Crystal Palace was attended by thousands of people. And in February Bell, in recognition of

58

his invention of the telephone, and Henry M. Stanley, the African explorer, were made life members of the Society of the Arts. Bell received the society's silver medal for his paper on the telephone. Earlier in January he received a telegram from Sir Thomas Biddulph, private secretary to Queen Victoria, asking when it would be convenient to demonstrate his telephone to Her Majesty at Osborne House. Mabel reported to her mother: "Alec replied that Thursday or Friday of next week would be most convenient, but awaited Her Majesty's commands—this last he put in much to my Republican disgust to show that he was the Queen's subject."[13]

Mabel needed a new dress and had already written her mother for advice. Alec insisted that if she were to have one at all it must be of the best. He agreed that she should have it made in Paris. Unfortunately, she was unable to go in person for fittings, but she urged her Paris dressmaker to finish it in time for her to wear to Osborne House. The dress and proposed visit proved to be a disappointment:

I know you are all waiting anxiously to hear all about our visit to the Queen, so I may as well begin by saying that Sir Thomas Biddulph has refused to permit me to accompany Alec. He says he doesn't see how it could be managed without asking Her Majesty and he does not like to do so. Well, I am disappointed, principally I think because it would be fine to write you about.

Alec goes down to Cowes on Saturday to see that all is in readiness as the presentation has been changed to Monday, and immediately afterwards, he leaves for Paris where he is to remain at least a week. I am anx-

ious to go too, it is so dreadfully dreary without him. I don't see how I can survive a week's solitary confinement as it will be.

I am justly indignant that the pains and labor bestowed in getting my dress ready for the Queen will be thrown away. It was not to have been finished until the 15th, but I wrote on Friday and it is promised for tomorrow. Do you know about the hardest part of not going to see the Queen is that you will all be disappointed.[14]

The black silk dress arrived from Paris:

Well, with some shortening of the train, you could wear it and not feel too gorgeous although it is heavily trimmed with jet. But I am afraid it is altogether too old for me. I am so vexed I could cry. I fear the blame for the dress lies entirely on me, but I did try not to say too much. I now see what a goose I was to use the words "long train" to a dressmaker but you used those words to me. I repeated them thinking it necessary to make the dressmaker understand what kind of dress I wanted.

I said my dress was for ceremonious calls and receptions; that I wanted a handsome dress but it must be very simple; I wanted something that would be handsome but not showy. Well, if it isn't a showy dress, I don't know what it is. What shall I do? I thought I was going to see the Queen and I knew I must have a dress even if I did not go. I think I did not use language descriptive enough but I feel so helpless and ignorant. The worst of the thing is the good round sum there will be to pay; I have about made up my mind not to buy a single new dress until you come.[15]

For the most part their London homelife was a source of pleasure to both Mabel and Alec:

I am afraid you didn't get as many letters as usual from me. I have no regular time for writing and always look forward to Sunday as the day set apart for letter writing.... We have not been to church regularly or often since we came here. First because it hurts Alec to sit still and then for one reason or another. Now he says I shall not go any more until after the baby is born. Alec considers Sunday emphatically his day of rest. He refuses to get out of bed until after ten. We have dinner at three and Colonel Reynolds comes every now and then and Mr. Holmes almost every Sunday evening bringing a friend or two with him; Chester Bell once in a long while. So you see we are not alone on Sundays. I like it, for it is like old times in Cambridge when your house was so full. We like Mr. Gaulie, a friend of Alec's, very much. Berta and Grace might laugh at him but he is very pleasant with plenty of talk and very careful always to speak to me so that I can understand what he says, which is more than most people take the trouble to do.[16]

Alec fully appreciated what it meant for Mabel to be separated from her family and he wrote to Mrs. Hubbard:

Mabel has hitherto been so much part of you that it seemed at first like tearing her life to pieces to remove her from your sheltering care. If there is anything that can console me for this cruelty, it is the feeling that the temporary separation has brought her nearer to me—that it has made us more truly man and

wife than we could ever have hoped to become in America—and that it has converted the helpless clinging girl into the self-reliant woman. Still, I think we both agree that we have had enough of separation and you will be assured that no mother could receive a more hearty welcome from her children than you will receive from us. [17]

Mrs. Hubbard came to London to be with Mabel when the baby was born. Bell was receiving so much acclaim in England for his invention of the telephone that Mrs. Hubbard was concerned in case Mabel became completely overshadowed by her distinguished husband. However, upon arriving in London she was delighted to see how Mabel had matured during her first year of marriage. Writing to Alec's mother, she said:

Mabel is looking so well. The house is simply furnished with exquisite taste; just the house in every respect that we could have wished for them and both are so happy and preside with so much ease and grace. Mabel was never half so charming and fascinating and as for Alec, you would be more proud of him than ever.

He has grown stouter—209 pounds and seems very well. His mornings are spent with his secretary or in his laboratory. He dines at seven and his evenings are given to Mabel. She retires about ten and he studies until one. Mabel superintends her household as quickly and with as much ease and self-reliance as though she had been mistress of a house for years. [18]

Mrs. Hubbard never lost her concern about Mabel's articulation, and while in London she urged Alec to continue his instruction to improve it. This he refused to do, maintaining that a husband and wife were equal and that equality was not compatible with the role of teacher and pupil.

The baby was born on May 8, 1878, and was called Elsie May. Mabel observed that although Alec was very fond of the new baby, he was afraid of the poor little thing, hardly knowing how to hold her. She also noted that he lost no time in checking to make certain her organs of speech, sight and hearing were perfect. In September Alec wrote: "I do love little children and I like nothing better than being among them. I can hardly wait for Elsie to quit the baby stage and be old enough for me to really love her."[19]

7
Storm Clouds

IN SPITE OF MRS. HUBBARD'S glowing picture of her daughter and son-in-law's domestic life, it was not quite as rosy as she painted it. Alec may have spent his evenings at home while she was visiting, but that was not always the case. Moreover, Mabel and Alec were concerned about their living expenses. They saw money disappearing without being quite sure how it was to be replaced. At first, Alec felt confident he could support them from fees received from his telephone lectures, but in time public interest in the novelty began to wane. The English telephone company that Colonel Reynolds hoped to establish failed to get sufficient capital. The Hubbards grew doubtful that Reynolds had been the right person to put in charge of such an undertaking. Mabel was concerned as Reynolds still owed Bell five hundred pounds on the British patents:

Well, I am glad that we have decided to go housekeeping for it will teach me the value of money and I think I will be more careful now. Oh Mama, to think of having to spend more than a hundred dollars and not being able to save a cent. Of course, I must have spoons and forks to eat with and salt cellars to hold the salt, sheets and table napkins are necessities and yet I can't bear to buy them for our money does run out fast and the balance is getting so low.

I know Alec is dreadfully anxious for some regular employment. If the English company could only be formed, they would have to refund five hundred pounds to us and that would make everything straight, especially if they give Alec the post of electrician, but we have heard little of it of late. I am sure Papa is right in saying that Alec is not suited to this work. Alec says he will not wait until his money is gone before he gets some more. Oh dear, I do wish the Bell Telephone Company would earn enough money to at least pay for all the time and work Alec put on the telephone last winter. It is so dreadful to see him worried and all his chances of working and improving the telephone gone for the present while he has to earn his bread and butter.[1]

Hubbard thought Colonel Reynolds should pay Alec for his services in introducing the telephone throughout England. Mabel was confident that he would. A few weeks later she was pleased to announce:

Colonel Reynolds yesterday gave Alec a check for the full amount he owes. Now Mama darling, I do hope you and Papa will feel better about Colonel Reynolds. The gentlemen were to have met yesterday to consider the terms of the new company and to settle everything. I fear something went wrong or there was some delay for Alec did not receive the telegram Colonel Reynolds promised to send.[2]

This letter foreshadows the conflict that was to erupt two years later between Bell and his father-in-law:

I am so sorry poor Papa has to work so hard. I really do not think there is any danger of Alec doubting how hard and faithfully Papa works for us all. If it seems so at any time, remember Alec was not well in health and anxious and worried in mind, distracted between his feverish anxiety to experiment and feeling that he could not do it for the want of a little money. Everything conspired to make him unreasonable and doubtful of everybody and everything but he is better now and I think Papa would be satisfied if he could know how much Alec loves and honors him.[3]

In spite of these strains on their marriage, Mabel was able to write that "Alec is just as loving as ever he could be and instead of finding more faults in him, as they say married people always find in each other, I only find more to love and admire. It seems to me I did not half know him when I married him."[4]

As early as February 1878, Mr. William Preece, the British electrical expert, accurately predicted other trials that would overshadow Bell's life when he wrote:

When once a new thing is shown to be true, a host of detractors delight in proving that it is not new. The inventor is shown to be a plagiarist or a purloiner or something worse.... Professor Bell will have to go through all this.[5]

Bell had already had such experiences in America and now letters were beginning to appear in *The Times* charging Bell with the theft of the telephone idea from Wheatstone or Reis. These letters did much to dampen the enthusiasm of prospective backers. An even more distressing event occurred in the late summer of 1878. Grey and Edison, in the interest of the Western Union, published insinuations against Bell's honor as an inventor. Bell was in Ireland when these scathing letters appeared in *The Times*. As Mabel was on her own, she had plenty of time to think about them and be disturbed:

I have been working all evening on my needlework and have plenty of time for thought which I have used to work myself up into such a state of indignation over that horrid letter in *The Times*. The more I think of it, the more it seems like a deliberate attempt not only to rob you of all credit in your own discovery, but also to convey the impression that you are a thief and purloiner of other men's ideas....

Altogether the article gives a most disagreeable impression of you and is a reflection on your honor which no man of any spirit could stand. For your own sake and for all our sakes, please do something. Cannot you write a note to the Editor and if he will not publish it, write to the *Telegraph* or some other paper that may be glad to take up anything against *The*

Times. **Don't you see how the unanswered insinuations of all these attacks must be injuring you in the eyes of all honest but imperfectly informed people. These attacks must keep back many who would only be too glad to receive you as the real discoverer of a great thing, but who would scorn to associate with an imposter.**[6]

As autumn approached, Bell grew increasingly bitter knowing how those letters distressed Mabel:

The more fame a man gets for an invention, the more does he become a target for the world to shoot at. I am beginning to be quite troubled too just because you are. Let the press quarrel over the inventor of the telephone if it pleases. Why should it matter to the world who invented the telephone as long as the world gets the benefit of it? Why should it matter to me what the world says upon the subject so long as I have obtained the object for which I labored and have got my sweet darling wife? And why should it matter so very much to you and to my little Elsie so long as the pecuniary benefits of the inventor are not taken from us— and so long as you are conscious of my uprightness and integrity?... Truth and Justice will triumph in the end. Let others vindicate my claim if they choose but keep me out of the strife.[7]

At this same time the Bell Company in America was suing the Western Union Telegraph Company and made repeated requests to Bell to file his statement, which he ignored. His attention was once again directed toward the teaching of the deaf by a plea for assistance in finding a teacher trained in visible speech for two or three deaf children in Greenock, Scotland. The teacher Bell recommended was unable to go so Bell went instead, probably welcoming the opportunity. Mabel may have been reacting to pressure from her parents to have Bell return to Boston, or possibly she simply resented his leaving her and their child for such an undertaking; at any rate, a letter from her brought this outburst from her husband:

I do not consider myself as working so many hours a day "for a couple of babies"—but as inaugurating a revolution in the methods of teaching deaf children in this country. I do not see in this school the two or three children actually present—but the 30,000 deaf mutes of Great Britain.... I trust that you will see that I am needed and my presence or absence may mean the success or failure of the new method of teaching articulation in this country. I have been waiting for months past for something to do. I have been absolutely rusting from inaction—hoping that my services might be wanted somewhere. Now I am needed and needed here. I am not going to forsake my little school just when it is struggling for existence—though the telephone should go to ruin—and though my wife and child should return to America and leave me here to work alone. I shall make this school a success if I have to remain until Christmas. It is a sorrow and grief to me that you have always exhibited so little interest in the work I have at heart—and that you have neither appreciated Visible Speech nor have encouraged me to work for its advancement.

Of one thing I am quite determined and that is to waste no more time and money on the telephone. If I

am to give away any more of my time—it must be for the object that is nearest my heart.... I am sick of the telephone and have done with it—excepting as a plaything to amuse my leisure moments. We cannot live for many months longer as we have been doing and I must go to work at something that will pay me and at the same time be doing some good in the world.

I never would have commenced to work on the telephone had it not been for the temptation of assistance from your father and Mr. Sanders. I never would have continued to work on the subject had it not been that I wished your father and Mr. Sanders to be repaid for the money they expended upon patents and upon my experiments. And I never would have succeeded in perfecting the telephone had it not been for the hope of getting you, my sweet wife; the struggle is ended now and I long for peace.... If my ideas are worth patenting, let others do it. Let others endure the worry, the anxiety and expense. I will have none of it. There is too much of the element of speculation in patents for me. A feverish anxious life like that I have been leading since our marriage would soon change my whole nature. Already it has begun injuring me and I feel myself growing irritable, feverish and disgusted with life.[8]

Bell decided that as he was no longer interested in the telephone company, he would leave England and go to Brantford, Ontario, to resume his teaching profession. His determination to concentrate on this and have nothing further to do with the telephone caused consternation among the other officers of the company. As Mabel's efforts to get him to submit his statement had so far failed, Hubbard suggested that Watson, Bell's former assistant, be sent to Quebec to meet their ship when it docked on November 10, 1878; perhaps Watson could persuade him to come to Boston. His task was not easy, but with Mabel's help he did manage to persuade Bell to return with him—but not before Bell took his wife and daughter to his father's home in Brantford. In a letter written to her mother, Mabel gave this picture of the situation:

Poor Alec has been suffering terribly since we landed, with abscesses. Yesterday and the day before he nearly fainted several times, and yesterday he had two shivering fits that frightened me very much. To-day he is suffering less or he could not have gone; but he is very weak and looks dreadful and I am frightened. Oh, if I could only be with him as I am so worried for the whole responsibility of his going is mine; he would not have gone but that I felt so strongly about it. But now that he is gone, Papa will be very kind to him, won't he? Alec is not like Papa, he cannot go on working steadily, and particularly through all suffering, as Papa does. He cannot help it if he is not so brave.[9]

On arrival in Boston, Bell had to go into the Massachusetts General Hospital. His preliminary statement, dated November 29, 1878, was made while he was there, but it was filed in time and thus saved the patent. Hubbard finally persuaded him to give up the idea of teaching in Canada and to remain in Boston with the company on a salary of $5,000 nominally as electrician but actually to assist counsel in the Bell Telephone Company's case against Western Union. Mabel was delighted when she heard the news and made plans to join her husband at the earliest opportunity.

8
Return to the United States

FOR A LITTLE WHILE after Mabel joined her husband in the United States toward the end of 1878, they lived in the Hubbard family home at Cambridge. The Hubbards were wintering in Washington, and Mabel longed to be there sharing the family life that she had missed so much while in England. Although the Bell Telephone Company was based in Boston, much of Bell's work assisting counsel in the pending case against Western Union would also be done in Washington. No matter in which city they chose to live, Alec would have to spend considerable time away from home. Although preferring Cambridge, he succumbed to the gentle family pressure and agreed to rent a home in Washington at 1509 Rhode Island Avenue, within walking distance of the Hubbard home.

So delighted was Mabel to be in daily contact with her parents and sisters again that she did not realize what a strain frequent periods of separation would put on their marriage; Alec recognized the problem at a very early stage:

Don't let us consent to being separated any more; help me darling to prevent it now. Let us lay it down as a principle of our lives that we shall be together, that we shall share each other's thoughts and lives—and to be to one another all that a husband and wife could be. Letters cannot speak as we can face to face—heart to heart. Separation must tend toward separation. Fragments of our lives must inevitably drop out of each other's knowledge if we are separated. In spite of daily interchange of written thought little by little the breach will widen until at length we lose the sense of unity of life and learn to live apart.[1]

This journal entry for March 1879 gives a picture of an ordinary day in Mabel's life:

Yesterday Alec left us for Boston, to be gone no one knows how long. It is all on account of that wretched lawsuit, the Bell Telephone Company versus the American Telephone Company, alias the Western Union Telegraph Company.

All day long he worked over old letters trying to find something that will throw light of any kind on the lawsuit, while his secretary copied references and I unpacked first one trunk and then another as the first proved too small to hold his big books.

Sitting on the floor in the midst of all the confusion I had created with drawers opened and their contents strewn all around on table, chairs and bed, Alec and I got into a long discussion on riches. I say I want fifteen thousand a year, my fine house and carriage.

Alec says five thousand a year is a handsome income and that I would be able to keep a carriage on that. "Well, if you want me to give up scientific work and devote myself to making money, you can probably lie in your carriage and dress in velvet, etc." "What is there higher than making money really?" asked I rebelliously with unfelt frivolity. "Science, adding to knowledge, bringing us nearer to God," answers he sitting upright and speaking enthusiastically. "Yes I hold that is the highest of all things, the increase of knowledge making us more like God. And will you bring me down and force me to give up my scientific work?" "No, only I want money too if I can get it." "So you shall my dear," declares my husband turning suddenly around, "and doubtless you will by and by."[2]

One of the hardest lessons Mabel had to learn in these early years of her marriage was to accept the fact that her husband could not work as other men did. Alec explained it to her:

I have my periods of restlessness when my brain is crowded with ideas tingling to my fingertips when I am excited and cannot stop for anybody. Let me alone, let me work as I like even if I have to sit up all night or even for two nights. When you see me flogging, getting tired, discouraged or my work done, then come in and stop me, make me lie down, put your hands over my eyes so that I go to sleep and let me sleep as long as I like until I wake. Then I may hang around, read novels and be stupid without an idea in my head until I get rested and ready for another period of work. But oh, do not do as you too often do, stop me in the midst of my work, my excitement with "Alec, Alec aren't you coming to bed? It's one o'clock, do come." Then I have to come feeling cross and ugly. Then you put your hands on my eyes and after awhile I go to sleep, but the ideas are gone, the work is never done.[3]

Mabel confided in her journal:

Well I will try and do better. I begin to think he is right myself; I know I have not acted with proper tact about the question of his going to bed regularly. Our worst quarrels have always been about that. No, the first rank belongs to the all important one of getting up in the morning but this follows close behind.[4]

Domestic arrangements in their London home had run comparatively smoothly thanks to the help of Mary Home, but although she came to America with them, Mabel found herself confronted with all sorts of domestic problems. Besides Mary, they brought an English nurse-maid, Annie, to care for Elsie. These English servants had difficulty adjusting to American life, particularly working with black servants. So it was almost a relief when Annie finally gave notice and returned to England. Mabel wrote of her problems:

It is hard living above a crater never knowing when the explosion may take place and I do long to see more of my little girl than Annie lets me. I want a good capable nurse for Elsie and nothing more, not one so very smart and knowing that I have nothing to do. I don't want things made easy for me. I would rather struggle through until I know how to make them easy for myself.[5]

Alec did little to help her in acquiring the experi-

74

ence she needed, and there must have been many times when he compounded the problem:

Alec has just come upstairs flourishing the poker and wanting to know what to do as the new servants have let the fires go out. A mild suggestion on my part that he may go down to the cellar and bring up some coal does not seem to meet with his approval. He is going to leave the fires as they are so that they may remember the next time.[6]

Against this picture of their domestic life there was also the absorbing social life of Washington. Mabel's entrance into Washington society was not without its attendant frustrations:

Alas for my hopes of a good time at Mrs. Pollok's party! Alec was summoned to Boston to a meeting of the stockholders of the New England Telephone Company and of course I could not make my first appearance in Washington Society without him. I hoped Alec might come home Friday and go with me to Mrs. Blaine's reception last night but no, a telegram said, "All working satisfactory, leave Monday night." I decidedly did not think it satisfactory.[7]

On rare occasions Alec accompanied Mabel on traditional afternoon calls, but these too were frustrating:

This afternoon I spent getting ready to make some calls. My maroon dress came home in time for me to wear it, but when Alec saw me in it he utterly refused to make calls with such a gorgeous person and I had to go down on my knees to him before he would hear of it, then to put on his things myself. By the time we got to Mama's it was pretty late and most of the

callers at the different receptions had gone.[8]

This item from Mabel's journal gives an insight into the social attitudes of the day:

Just returned from a reception at Senator Sherman's. Mrs. Lander was there and told Alec apropos of his question as to when [Sir Henry] Irving would be here, that she hoped no one would make the mistake of inviting Ellen Terry to meet him; that recently in New York Irving asked permission to bring her to a home to which he had been invited, and was told that his host would be glad to see her but the ladies would be out! Such a mean thing to do or say. Because of a fault committed years ago and repaired as far as possible by devoted care of her children Miss Terry is to be excluded from all good society while Irving, about whose past there are stories and who is certainly divorced from his wife, is received and feted everywhere. The reply I suppose would be, if you think so, why don't you invite her to your house? I would privately but not publicly for this reason, that my own position in society is not yet secure and I have no right to injure my husband or children for what after all would be no pleasure to her. I wouldn't go out of my way to be polite to her or to anyone else in her position but I don't think I would insult her. I do think our laws are so hard on women in such cases.

Some time ago talking of divorce, Alec said he did not believe in it when there were children. I asked would he force a lady to live with her husband if she knew him to be a libertine? He said no, he would have no divorce granted but he would have the gentleman

76

put in prison. Think what a sensation that would make, a gentleman at hard labor! I think it would have a more deterrent effect upon gentlemen villains than legal separation from a woman of whom they were tired.[9]

During the summer of 1878 while the Bells were in England, Hubbard had gone through a financial crisis that had repercussions on the telephone companies in America. Stockholders of both the New England Telephone Company and the Bell Telephone Company lost confidence in his management and did not wish him to continue as president of either company. Alec became involved in the controversy. He wrote Mabel:

I am troubled and anxious and don't know what to do. I love your father and am proud of him as head of this Company—and yet even I feel that his name stands in the way of our obtaining the financial support we require and threatens financial ruin to the Company. I wish you would put your arms around my neck and tell me what you wish.[10]

It was not until February of the following year, when the Bells were in Washington, that the matter was finally settled by a reluctant Hubbard relinquishing his office of president, although he remained on the board of directors. Mabel described a call made with her mother on Mrs. Howe, the wife of one of the men involved in the company reshuffle:

For an hour poor little Mama sat and talked, hearing Mrs. Howe's complaints, explaining things, admitting others, and generally managing to cheer Mrs. Howe and get the blame off Papa's shoulders. I told her I thought it was a shame she had to do all the

comforting, not only for her own family but everybody else besides; she had to carry the burden of cheering the whole Bell Telephone Company on her shoulders and no one to comfort her. I never realized before how much she helped Papa, standing by his side ready to defend him and explain and smooth the ruffled feelings of those who may feel hurt by anything he may have done.[11]

Mabel was concerned for her father during this power play, but became even more concerned for her husband when she learned that the next proposed move was to turn Bell out of the company. Some members believed that he had stumbled on the telephone by accident and was unlikely to come up with any further inventions. Mabel wrote to Alec: "I cannot sit quietly by and see you pushed out of your own concern and they will not dare do so if you can only bring out something no matter what."[12]

Bell appreciated and shared her concern:

Oh Mabel dear, please, please, make me describe and publish my ideas that I may at least obtain credit for them and that people may know that I am still alive and thinking. I can't bear to hear that even my friends should think that I have stumbled upon an invention and that there is no more good in me. You are the mistress of my heart and sharer of my thoughts (haven't I become poetical?) so I send you a few ideas—as they come to me—to be added to the list of unwritten inventions and upon my return to be written out by US my dear.[13]

Around this time Bell decided to write a history of his research work in electric telephony, believing such a book would establish his reputation as an inventor for all time. He suggested that Mabel should sell some of her telephone shares to support them while he worked on his book, and when it was published the proceeds should be hers. Mabel's journal contains this reaction to his suggestion:

I must confess I do not like to live on my capital; if I could invest in some paying concern and live on the interest, I should be only too glad to agree but I don't know what is more important just now, the book or a new invention. However, if what is rumored is true, that Mr. Edison has gone to Europe, that leaves us in peace for awhile and I know however hard and faithfully Alec may work on his book, he cannot prevent ideas entering and overflowing his brain.[14]

When summer arrived, they gave up the house in Washington and returned to the Hubbard home in Cambridge. Although Mabel was pregnant at the time, they lived a busy life surrounded by family. This became the general pattern for many future summers:

This has been a very busy summer for us all. Lena and Augusta [McCurdy cousins] have been here since the beginning of July and I now find that their father has shut up his house leaving them on my hands until September without a "by your leave." Then Papa and Sister are in England, the one on Telephone business, the other to see and enjoy all she missed last year. Mama, Berta, and Augusta going off on short visits to the seaside now and then. Now at last Grandpa [McCurdy] has come and right glad I am to see him for his own sake. He is very feeble.[15]

When the summer was over, they returned to Washington, taking up residence at 904-14th Street, N.W.

Her sister Gertrude had a whirlwind romance and became engaged at Christmas, 1879, to Maurice Grossman from New York, a Hungarian who had started his career as an actor and then decided to study law. Mabel described him and the subsequent wedding to Alec's mother:

I wanted to tell you all about my "Hungarian brother" as he calls himself, as our heads and hearts were so full of him and my sister but I could not manage it. Now I will only say "he came, saw and conquered." He was so cordial, so friendly and determined to love all my sister's family and friends. He is so full of life, love and boyish spirits that it was quite impossible to do otherwise than like him.[16]

I have been waiting until after the wedding to tell you the whole story. I suppose Alec told you why they changed their minds so suddenly. Maurice found it would take him at least five years to qualify as a lawyer and they were neither of them young enough to wait all that time. Maurice could easily make plenty of money by acting, but neither he nor Papa wanted him to do that, so at last it was decided that he should go to Germany as head of the International Telephone Company, a new Company which Papa started. Maurice had of course little acquaintance with the business details of the organization of companies, but he has many influential friends in the chief European capitals and in many ways will be of much assistance to the business managers. He is very much interested in the tele-

phone and a very clever, clearheaded man and we all think he will do very well. The managers were to start last Saturday and Maurice had to go out at the same time if he wanted the position. He refused to go without Sister nor would she let him, so a week ago Sunday it was decided and Saturday she was married.

Such a breathless race it was to get everything ready. Two hundred and fifty "At Home" cards to be ordered, addressed and sent out with only two days' notice, wedding dresses to be ordered from New York and made up in the same length of time, presents bought, friends invited and received and housed here, there and everywhere, flowers brought from Cambridge and arranged, etc., etc. And all was done and ready by 8:00 P.M., only half an hour late![17]

Shortly after all the excitement of Sister's wedding, Mabel gave birth to her second daughter on February 15. Again she wrote to Mrs. Bell:

I am on the sofa for the first time this morning and must try and give you an account of my little one, as I fear Alec has been far too busy with his baby [the invention of the electric photophone] to talk or write much about mine. What his baby is I leave him to tell you, sufficient to say, he thinks it more wonderful than the telephone, though he cannot assert it is more marvelous than this little living, human mite lying so quietly in her dainty blue and white bed by my side. My little girl has long thick black hair but is not so dark as Elsie, though still far from fair. Even Alec, who could not endure my poor little Elsie at this age, thinks her pretty. I want to name her Marian Hubbard but am

81

not perfectly sure that Mama likes it. It was the name of my youngest sister; she says yes, but so quietly I am waiting to see if she can stand it after a day or two's trial.[18]

This child was christened Marian Hubbard, but was always called Daisy.

By April 15 of that year Mabel's younger sister Berta became engaged to Charlie Bell, a cousin of Alec's who lived with them as Alec's secretary until a better place could be found for him in the telephone company.

Shortly after his marriage, Bell had placed his rights in the English telephone company in a trust for the benefit of any children they might have and had made Hubbard the sole trustee. Hubbard went to England in the summer of 1878 to reorganize the faltering English telephone company. He succeeded in obtaining $12,000 in cash for the trust and stock in the reorganized firm. By the following summer it was worth $100,000. On his return, still going through what proved to be his last financial crisis, he obtained Bell's reluctant permission to borrow cash from the trust fund for his personal use. This, together with the fact that Hubbard as trustee never discussed the details of his administration of the trust with Bell, nearly caused a complete rupture in the Bell-Hubbard family.

At first, in an attempt to avoid such a situation, Bell simply refused to discuss the trust, no doubt giving Hubbard the impression that his son-in-law had no interest in the matter. Being uncommunicative by nature, it never occurred to him to give anyone information unasked. Consequently, a wall of silence grew up between the two men. Finally, when Bell could stand it no longer, he wrote a long letter to his father-in-law that showed clearly that, in his opinion, the trust had been mishandled.

Hubbard was deeply hurt and strongly defended his position, reminding his son-in-law that had he not salvaged the failing English company there would have been little or nothing in the trust. This conflict between the two men they loved most dearly distressed Mabel and her mother. Mrs. Hubbard was angry and indignant, while Mabel expressed her opinion by writing to Alec: "My Darling, your letter is honorable to you but it was written hastily and it was unjust to another."[19]

She then wrote another letter to her mother explaining Alec's position:

He thinks it is far better to be perfectly frank and open and he is perfectly willing to admit that Papa may be entirely in the right but he does want to have the opinion of some other business person. His greatest concern is not what was done or not done but simply that Papa never volunteers any information concerning the affairs of the Trust.... Well, I have found out for myself that Alec is a very hard man to deal with. The only thing I can do is make the best of matters but you may be sure that there is no one more true and loving than he in spite of everything.[20]

The open conflict may have cleared the air between the two men, but the hurt remained for a long time, as evidence in this letter Mabel later wrote to Alec:

Did you read Mama's letters? Somehow they all left a feeling of sadness in my mind, especially any reference to my dear father. I feel as though Mama were half unconsciously and indirectly trying to change

what she feels is your unjust opinion of Papa. I may be all wrong but it does seem to me as if Mama were unhappy about you and Papa and poor little Mama has much to bear and worry her. I feel as if they were both trying very hard to do everything they could for you.

Oh Alec Dear, if you would but write to them. If not to Papa because of the questions that must be opened, then to Mama. Just a bright kind loving playful letter such as you write to me so often. Nothing I could do or say would give her so much pleasure as that. Please do my Darling for my sake and for hers. She has done so much for you and you do not know how she loves you. I don't believe she could love you more if you were her own son.[21]

Alec must have followed Mabel's advice, for the painful breach in their relationship was healed and for the rest of their lives a bond of love and understanding existed between the two families.

9
Family Life

THE HUBBARD FAMILY WENT TO EUROPE in 1881 and remained several years. Hubbard, assisted by his sons-in-law, Maurice Grossman and Charles Bell, was trying to establish telephone companies in various European countries. Alec and Mabel accepted Hubbard's invitation to use the Cambridge house for the summer with delight. Mabel wrote her mother:

> In the old house again, welcomed by yours and Papa's cable and note. It is so lovely to be here again and yet so sad. All around marks of your presence and yet you are not here. Alec and I love this old house so very much and are so glad to have our children here that they may love it too.... I think it feels more really home to Alec than our own home.[1]
>
> How did you manage to exist here all alone when Papa was in Washington? My husband is in Washington now and he too promises to have his work done in a fortnight. Will he keep his promise as well as Papa did his I wonder? To think that I am "Mama" now in the place where I was a little girl, that my babies run around where I ran, sit in the same high-chair at table, and play about the same games as I did—I can hardly realize it all.
>
> If I could be as much to my children as you have been to me my mother—I am getting rather anxious about it—Elsie says so little to me and so much more to

others. She very evidently sees the difference and points out things to me instead of saying them. I fear she may learn to give her confidence and tell her little stories to others until it will be too late for her to care to come to me with them. I know she is fonder of me than anyone else but she does not talk to me as she does to others—from what her nursemaid says, she must be full of childish prattle and pretty dictatorial ways—all of which I see nothing as she talks so indistinctly, hardly moving her lips.[2]

Alec did keep his promise on that occasion and returned for what he hoped would be a quiet, restful summer. That hope was shattered suddenly on July 2, 1881, with the shooting of President James A. Garfield by Charles J. Guiteau, a deranged office-seeker. Like the whole American nation, the Bells were shocked. The wounded president was hurried back to the White House from the Washington, D.C., railway station. No one knew whether he would live or die, or where the bullet had lodged. Röntgen's discovery of X-rays still lay fourteen years in the future.

Bell had carried out experiments in England in 1878, attempting to invent an electric probe to locate metal in the human body. Although it was never successfully completed, he offered the idea and his services to the president's physicians. Professor Newcomb of the Smithsonian Institution worked frantically with other distinguished scientists and Bell's own associate, Professor Trainer, to produce an instrument that would locate the bullet in the president's body. Mabel explained to Alec's mother:

Alec I have hardly seen the last few days, he has

86

been hard at work day and night on an apparatus for the use of the President's physicians. He thought he would have it finished and be off to Washington last night but alas an accident happened and from the heights Alec has gone down to the depths. However, he has gone to work again and hopes perhaps to get off tonight.[3]

As the summer was so hot in Cambridge, Mabel and the children went to the seaside at Pigeon Cove, Massachusetts. From there she followed Alec's progress in the press, writing regularly to encourage him:

I cannot begin to tell you how anxiously I watch for news of you and your doings, how you are succeeding. Oh, how I hope you will be able to find the bullet, it would be such a triumph for you. Of course I want it for the President's sake also but I want you to be the man to do it, my own dear boy.[4]

Finally, Bell considered his probe sufficiently developed to try it on the president. He warned the physicians about removing all metal objects from the vicinity of the bed. Unfortunately, through an oversight a steel coil mattress under the hair mattress caused so much electrical interference that the experiment failed. When Mabel learned of it, she tried to encourage her husband:

You poor boy, how sorry I am for you in your disappointment. I can imagine just how chagrined and mortified you must have felt when those horrid noises [from the steel coils in the bottom mattress] prevented you being sure what you heard. Never mind, courage; from failure comes success, be worthy of your patient and don't lose heart even if all others are discouraged. I have not the least doubt but that you will eventually succeed. You have never yet failed and will not now. Only I wish I could be with you to help try to cheer you. If it were not for the little ones, I would come right down.

How excited you must have been to go into the President's bedroom. Thank you very much for telling me all about it and taking so much pains to draw the plan of the room. I almost feel as if I had been there too. I am glad you admired the President so much. Don't you think he will live? I wish you had seen Mrs. Garfield too; she must be so brave to keep up through everything as she does. Oh dear, why couldn't I have been invisible to see everything too but I don't know but that I prefer you to tell me about it.[5]

Two days later she wrote:

I am sorry I did not write you yesterday but I sent a telegram instead. I am so glad to hear that you are improving your apparatus. I hope the second attempt will be successful. I know you deserve it and poor Mr. Garfield must wish it. I have been looking over the old papers of the first few days of Garfield's illness and wonder how he lived through them. There seems to have been so much confusion and everybody who liked had admittance to him. At one time it seemed that the whole Cabinet called upon him and all their wives were his nurses. I should think all that crowd would literally have worried him to death. My heart and mind are constantly occupied with you and the wish for Mr. President's recovery and I long to have you near to tell me all about it. No wonder you are exhausted and headachy. I only hope it won't make your nervous trouble worse.[6]

To Bell's dismay the president's health did not permit a second attempt. This failure to locate the bullet laid Bell open to mortifying criticism in the press. Probably never in his life did he do anything with less thought of personal gain and never anything for which he was more widely ridiculed. By October his apparatus was perfected and used successfully in New York. Several years later the University of Heidelberg bestowed a rare honorary doctorate of medicine degree on Bell for his contribution to surgery with this device.

As a final irony, while Bell had been struggling in Washington to save the president's life, his first son, Edward, was born prematurely at Pigeon Cove on August 15 with a breathing difficulty. He lived several hours and, being otherwise strong and healthy, might have pulled through if regular breathing could have been established. A year later, seeing Chester Arthur, Garfield's successor, in the casino in Newport, Mabel wrote wistfully: "How I wish he [Garfield] had lived. I feel as if though but for Guiteau our own lives might have been different; you might not have gone to Washington but have stayed with me and all might have been well."[7] Alec expressed his own grief in a very practical way—he set to work inventing a vacuum jacket machine for artificial respiration.

By September they decided to join the Hubbard family in Europe. Mabel felt she must justify her reasons for going to Alec's mother:

You know Alec has not been well for nearly a year past and the doctors say entire rest from mental labor is necessary to avert serious constitutional trouble. We hoped he would take this rest this summer but

the President's illness prevented it. While in Washington he seemed better but on his return, he felt the effects of the long excitement and my illness coming on top of that has thrown him completely back and our physician says he resumes his winter's work at his peril; that a journey in Europe with an ocean between him and his work will do more to restore him to complete health than anything else.

Though I have been very well, I am not yet strong, in fact I have had to go back to bed twice and am still there now. The Doctor says it will be some months before I can hope to regain complete strength. So for me too, he advises European travel. My children are just the age for such a journey, too young to mind the travel and yet not so young but that I can leave them with Mama for days at a time while we go off alone. In all probability I shall never have such a chance to travel until my children are grown up and married. Alec will never go without me so that in every way this seems too good an opportunity to be lost; especially as my family are in Europe and may be there for years and I may not see them otherwise. As Alec says, we now have money enough to do it and never may again as with each year our expenses increase and soon we shall have houses to maintain. It was he who proposed this plan. I have wanted to go for a long time to revisit the scenes I saw many years ago and I want to see my family but once I am at home again and know they are coming too, I shall never want to cross the ocean again.

At this point in the letter Alec added a P.S.:

What never? Hardly ever. Dear Mama don't believe half my little girl has said. I am all right although I need rest, but a European tour is a thing Mabel and I longed to make and as she says, we do not know when we may be able to go again.[8]

On their arrival in England they visited Mrs. Hubbard and Mabel's two sisters, who were both expecting babies, then joined her father in Paris. Alec was again being honored by the French government for his invention of the telephone with the Diploma of Honor, having received their Volta Prize the previous year.

Mabel loved revisiting Paris and seeing all the scenes that she had enjoyed as a young girl. But much as she reveled in the shops, she missed her mother and sisters. As she explained to her mother in London:

I am overwhelmed at the idea of getting my own clothes alone, what shall I do? I am making decidedly more use of Alec's Secretary [Mr. Johnson] than Alec is just now, as he goes on all shopping expeditions with me. If I took Alec he would be sure to have a bad attack of heart trouble in the first shop and make me buy all I didn't want. At present, not being bothered, he is very well. Just now he has gone off hunting for caterpillars as he had an idea that he can find a method of preventing them climbing trees! Alec says I am to have a dress from Worth's, but I think I will get Papa to take me there as Alec would never let me set a price or bother about how the dress is to be made. And yet, no one is more critical of the effect when finished.[9]

Their days of financial insecurity were finally past. In November 1879, Western Union had agreed to give up the telephone business on the advice of its counsel, who insisted that Bell's patent claims could not be defeated. Accordingly, in exchange for 20 percent of its customer telephone rental receipts over the next seventeen years, all Western Union telephone patents and related business were turned over to the Bell Telephone Company. Over an eighteen-year period the Bell patents were tested in some six hundred separate cases, comprising 149 volumes of printed records. The Bell Company won them all.

Bell wrote his father in 1880 that their income from all American sources had reached $24,000 a year. "We should be able to live on that," he commented wryly.

When the original Bell Company was reorganized into the American Bell Telephone Company in 1880, its 73,500 shares were exchanged on a six for one basis with those of the earlier company. Mabel owned 2,975 of the new shares. Any residual monies were invested in bank and railroad stocks.

In 1881 Bell sold nearly a third of their remaining telephone stock and placed the proceeds in U.S. bonds. An inventory taken in 1883 showed their American investments—excluding the more than $100,000 in the trust fund—to be worth $900,000 and bringing them an annual income of roughly $37,000. At a time when a loaf of bread cost two cents and a housemaid earned twenty-five cents a day plus room and board, Alexander Graham Bell had become a millionaire at thirty-six.

Such a sum, by contemporary standards, would equal fifty million dollars in purchasing power with no income tax! Incredibly, it had all been accomplished in seven years. They hadn't joined the league of Vanderbilts,

Morgans or Astors, but they had done very well for themselves nonetheless.

The Bells and their children remained in Europe until May 1882, then returned to Newport for the summer in her grandfather McCurdy's old home. From there Mabel wrote her mother in Europe: "We are going fishing this afternoon. I wish I had someone to go with Alec as I don't feel very enthusiastic but fear that Alec might go to sleep and tumble off the cliff if somebody does not look after him."[10]

Later, they returned to Washington and bought a large house at 1500 Rhode Island Avenue. Together with grounds, it occupied an entire block on Scott Circle. However, extensive renovations were needed, and these took the best part of a year to complete. Their new home included an oratory with a stained-glass window, a billiard room, library, a music room with a grand piano for Bell and a large conservatory. By October of the following year they were anxious to move in, but the workmen were still at work. Mabel wrote in her journal:

Alec told me not to work so hard but what was I to do—the moment I left the men an instant some mistake was made and the work had to be done all over again. The children caught cold and I got up night after night to assure myself they were all right and properly tucked in. I caught cold myself, had a cough for the first time in my married life. Alec went to the meeting of the National Academy in Hartford. Mama went to New York on a shopping expedition. I sent for the doctor who thought nothing of my cold, merely told me to be careful of drafts.... Was awakened in the morning by Elsie's kiss to find myself cold and shivering and

feverish. The doctor sent me to bed but assured me it was all right and there was no danger of my [expected] baby. Sister came and insisted on staying all night. After a rather restless night, about two I called Sister and thought she had better send for the doctor as I was not feeling well. Well, he was out so I sent over to my neighbor, Mrs. Poe, to ask if she knew of another physician nearby. She did not but came herself, and she it was who was my true friend in time of need, doing all for me and my poor little one that a physician could have done. Poor little one, it was so pretty and struggled so hard to live, opened his eyes once or twice to the world and then passed away. The little one whom we called Robert came November 17th.... Alec knew nothing of what had happened until he reached Washington three hours after my baby had come and gone and Mama not until the evening.

What we should have done without Mrs. Poe, my poor Sister and I cannot bear to think, the only wonder was that Sister was not ill herself, not being strong naturally and borne down by long anxiety about her husband. Poor Maurice, he grows weaker all the time. When I was able to be on the sofa, he and Sister went to Philadelphia, leaving their baby for the first time, and met the physicians in consultation there. The doctors decided that he was suffering from a tumor which could not be removed without killing him.[11]

Maurice died on October 16, 1884, at the age of forty-one. Here is how Mabel described her Hungarian brother-in-law:

He found it hard to go. He was so intensely alive.

We seem such a quite ordinary family now. Alec is a man out of the ordinary certainly but he is quieter in general life. He never shocks and takes away our pride with his overflowing spirits and utter disregard of conventionalities as Maurice sometimes did. We are all so quiet-mannered and self-restrained. He must have been like a breath of fresh air to my Sister, all her life more or less an invalid [tuberculosis]. I think he must have carried her completely by storm. He needed her so much, needed her calm almost masculine judgment, her strength of mind. She needed him so much, his constant tender watchfulness and care of her and his bright and joyous spirits to bring brightness to a life before rather sad and quiet.[12]

Sometime later she wrote:

Grace and I were talking of marrying again. I said if my husband died before I was very old, I might marry again, feeling the world and the care of my children and property too much for me, but I did not approve of it at all. Grace said she didn't see how they managed in heaven, that even if Sister wanted to, she did not see how she could marry again after having been Maurice's wife. It would drive him perfectly frantic to have her care for anyone else. He was a man who could be very jealous, who must have all of his wife's love or none.[13]

Maurice died without a will, so according to the prevailing intestate succession laws all his real estate and two-thirds of his personal estate went to his heir, who in this case was his only daughter, Gertrude, whose pet name was Gypsy. Had she not survived him, this portion of the estate would have gone to his parents as his next-of-kin rather than to his wife. Mabel shared her sister's consternation, as this journal entry revealed:

Sister said to Mama: "Gypsy cannot have this house. I cannot let her have it. I shall hate her, I know I should, if I thought she had Maurice's home." She does not know the further storm in store for her, his jewelry, his books and such things which have value only for him and her are also not hers. It seems to me almost more bitter than death, at least to add a terrible sting to it. It has come so fearfully home to me what suffering there may lie in the neglect to make a will that I have induced my own husband to go upstairs into his study and draw up a will. I hope as I write these lines he is writing his will. He is safe enough for I have made my will leaving him everything I have.

Alec has just brought me his will signed and witnessed. Now I am wondering if the document is legal being written on Sunday. Alec says: "Yes I am glad you did make your will but I would not have asked you to do so." Perhaps not, but he would have regretted not doing so all the rest of his life if he survived me. My making my will meant the loss or gain to him of more than half a million; his making his will gives me the privilege justly mine of carrying out his wishes which I certainly know better than anyone else and which would be more sacred to me than to anyone else. God knows I hope it will never be needed.[14]

Hubbard bought Maurice's home and its contents from the estate and gave it to his beloved daughter. However, she was not destined to enjoy it very long as she died two years after her husband, leaving her little daughter Gypsy to be brought up by the Hubbards.

Mabel's journal described Gertrude:

Sister was the cleverest of us all with much of Papa's intellect. Both Mama and Papa leaned much on her and depended on her judgment. Mama and she were very close to each other in those years in Germany when Mama was so often ill and Papa away and the rest of us too young to help. Afterwards Sister was always Papa's companion on his many long journeys in connection with the Railway Mail Committee.[15]

Tragedy again struck the Hubbard family when Berta, who had also suffered from tuberculosis, died in childbirth on July 4, 1885, leaving two little girls, Helen and Gracie. Mabel observed in her journal:

Berta and I had very little to do with each other after my illness as a child. She was too active and practical. I am inclined to romantic fancies with which her practical mind had no sympathy.

When she was fourteen she caught the measles, being the last of us to have them and although she was not very sick, it was succeeded by that terrible trouble tuberculosis which now after twelve years has cut short her beautiful young life. She had exquisite coloring, big saucer eyes and soft cheeks breaking into dimples when she laughed.[16]

When Bell returned from England in 1878, his major role with the telephone company was to assist in the litigation against the Western Union Telegraph Company. It was not until the late 'nineties that he was entirely free of the demands of counsel in the company's long fight against infringers. Year after year he was summoned, sometimes from abroad, for cross-examination on all the old evidence. But eventually with their new wealth Bell was able to follow his own pursuits. Mabel assumed full responsibility for their family life while Alec pursued his career.

One of the things he undertook was a research project for the Massachusetts State Board of health on the heredity of deafness. He delivered four papers to the Academy of Science on this subject, and went on during the 'eighties to trace deafness through several generations of certain selected families. The Lovejoy family, as an example, was traced from its Massachusetts progenitor in 1644 to its numerous branches in his own day. Limiting his research to New England, over a period of many years he and his assistants researched the history of every family reported to have had two or more deaf children.

This note delivered to Mabel by a hotel messenger gives an indication of his enthusiasm for the project:

Success at last, I believe I have now found the solution of my Lovejoy problem. Following up indications obtained from the Census Returns, I went to the Congressional Library to hunt up any town histories concerning places where my Lovejoys had lived. The last book I looked at was a History of Amherst, N.H., and there I found what I believe to be the ancestry of all my deaf mutes with his descent from John Lovejoy of Andover.

I feel as jealous of my book as a starving dog with a bone. I don't know where I can be safe from intrusion while I study it—so I have secured a room—

where I won't tell you. I send this note so that you may not be alarmed by my absence. Don't wait dinner if I am not back in time. May remain out until ten.[17]

Mabel did not share Alec's enthusiasm for genealogy, for on returning from Sunday afternoon tea at the Hubbard home she wrote in her journal:

Alec talked genealogy all the time. He thinks that in the course of a hundred years material will be gathered through Genealogical Societies from which important deductions can be made affecting the human race. I am afraid I am not particularly interested in investigations that can only be used a hundred years hence.[18]

Even Alec realized that this absorption in his work was separating him from his family circle:

My deaf-mute researches have taken me away— far away—from you all. I don't think your thoughts or feel your feelings—nothing but deaf-mutes—deaf-mutes—and solitude of mind. And the worst of it is that I don't see the end of it. I can't give up my investigations without finalizing them—or myself—and I don't see any prospect of either. Yet while my thoughts run in the deaf-mute line—I am practically banished from the family.[19]

In spite of his preoccupation with his deaf-mutes, Mabel made the most of those rare moments when she had his undivided attention:

Alec and I walked home and as it was too dark for Alec to talk to me, I had a good time talking to him about some letters I received. I do not very often feel that I have so much of my husband's attention as I did

tonight, he is usually so full of other things, but tonight it was too dark for Alec to talk to me so I had things all my own way.[20]

10
Discovering Baddeck

ALEC AND MABEL HAD PLANNED a European trip in the summer of 1885, but with Berta's imminent death hanging over them, they postponed their plans. Later in the summer they decided to take Alec's father, Melville Bell, with them to Newfoundland. When Hubbard learned of the plan, he urged them to break their journey in Nova Scotia's Cape Breton Island and visit the Caledonia coal mines, in which he had a long-standing financial interest.

They welcomed Hubbard's suggestion, particularly when Mrs. Hubbard assured Mabel she had never seen such beautiful fir trees growing anywhere else in the world. From Halifax they took a train to the Strait of Canso, separating Cape Breton Island from the mainland of Nova Scotia, then changed to a paddle steamer, the S.S. *Marion*, and sailed into the beautiful land-locked sea known as the Bras d'Or Lakes. Eventually, they reached the little village of Baddeck where they tied up at the wharf for the night. Mabel and the children were content to remain in their stateroom, but Alec wanted to explore the village. He had read *Baddeck and That Sort of Thing* by Charles Dudley Warner, a distinguished American writer who made the long arduous trip by coach a decade before and then wrote of his experiences.

Warner had stayed at the "Telegraph House" and had praised its hospitality and the charm of the "beautiful Maud," the proprietor's daughter. The proprietress, Mrs. Dunlop, made Bell welcome and provided him with a good meal. She was interested to learn that Bell was on his way to Newfoundland because she had originally come from there. At that moment the superintendent of the cable company arrived to inspect the telegraph office located in a room at the rear of the hotel. Accompanied by the attractive young girl who operated the telegraph office, they passed through the dining room while Bell was eating. In answer to Bell's inquiry, Mrs. Dunlop informed him that the girl was her daughter Maud. Alec could hardly wait to get back to the *Marion* and tell Mabel that he had seen "the beautiful Maud."

Next day they continued their voyage to Sydney and on to the Caledonia mines. After inspecting the mines they boarded the S.S. *Hanoverian* for Newfoundland. Near the end of the voyage the ship ran ashore on the treacherous Newfoundland coast. Everyone was rescued and brought to the fishing village of Portugal Cove. The sullen natives were not overjoyed by their arrival. Few carts were available, so most of the passengers walked eight miles to the next community and crowded into a small hotel for the night. They were picked up the following morning by boat and brought to St. John's. Mabel wrote to her mother:

We found all St. John's on the wharf waiting to see the shipwrecked passengers land, but they must have been disappointed for although nearly everyone owned only the clothes they stood up in, they looked very respectable, Alec especially, who is fast developing into a dandy in his old age.[1]

After a short visit in St. John's, they made their way back to Baddeck and spent the rest of their holiday at the Telegraph House. Years later, Maud Dunlop recalled meeting Mabel:

It was on their return visit to Baddeck that I first saw Mrs. Bell, at this time in her late twenties, a slender person with the gentlest manners, her sweet sympathetic face framed in the most beautiful soft brown hair. She and her two dark-eyed little girls made a lovely picture; they were most devoted to her. Even now, after so many years, I can see her sitting on the upper veranda reading aloud to them while their governess was out. She and Mr. Bell occupied their time during their stay in exploring the country around Baddeck, walking, driving and boating.[2]

Mabel caught Baddeck's peaceful magic when she wrote:

Baddeck is certainly possessed of a gentle restful beauty and I think we would be content to stay here many weeks just enjoying the lights and shade on all the hills and isles and lakes but I cannot see why C.D. Warner should be possessed of such a mad desire to come here that he must travel so uncomfortably day and night for thirty-six hours to spend two days here. No wonder the good people here took him for insane

and his friend for his keeper. May it be long before fashionable people with their big hotels, big trunks and high charges find their way here.[3]

Although Bell had become an American citizen and was most enthusiastic about everything American, he disliked the climate of his adopted country. All his life he suffered in hot weather and was subject to prickly heat. In Baddeck, although it might be hot in summer, there was always a cool breeze off the water. During September and October the air smelled like wine and the foliage blazed with color. Apart from its climate, the landscape reminded him of Scotland. The people too were Scots for the most part, emigrants from the terrible highland clearances when so many crofters were driven from their homes to make room for sheep. At the time of the Bells' arrival in Baddeck, many local people spoke only Gaelic. This all contributed to Bell's dream of having a cottage by a running brook where he and Mabel would be free from the pressures of city living and able to teach their children to enjoy life's simpler pleasures.

After returning to Washington, Bell wrote to Mrs. Dunlop, saying that they wished to come back and would like a cottage of their own. Upon their arrival the following summer, Mrs. Dunlop introduced them to Arthur McCurdy, a member of one of Baddeck's leading merchant families. He found a cottage for them on the shores of the Baddeck Bay a few miles from the village. Although it did not have the running brook that Alec so desired, it did have a good beach, a grove of pine trees and a fine view. They called their new home Crescent Grove. It was just a small farmhouse when they bought it, but later they enlarged it by jacking it up and building another storey underneath.

Baddeck had little in the way of furniture beyond the bare necessities, so Alec and Mabel had fun improvising. They made a chaise lounge from a wooden armchair, a box and a mattress stuffed with hay; barrel staves held together with rope became a hammock; boxes covered with cretonne served for shelves and tables.

A cow and a churn were acquired for making butter. Mabel described their first attempt at churning:

Yesterday after Alec returned we had our first churn. We all worked, Alec, the children and I, Alec especially, and after a long hard bout we had the delight of seeing butter form. It did look like tightly scrambled eggs at first but Nellie [the governess] who seems to know everything, soon brought it into shape and such beautiful yellow butter as it became. I wish you could have a taste of it. You see it is the very best butter made from the cream of a Jersey cow. But we found the churning process less delightful in practice than in theory and Alec is trying to invent a windmill to do our churning for us.[4]

Until his invention was completed, the children were encouraged to churn to the music of "Onward Christian Soldiers" vigorously played on the organ by their father.

During their first summer at Crescent Grove, Charlie Bell visited them. He and Alec discovered a waterfall on the Kenneth MacDermid farm on the opposite shore. Eventually, Bell purchased twenty acres of this property, which included the waterfall. A dream began taking shape in the minds of Alec and Mabel, a dream of owning the entire headland across the bay from Baddeck known as Red Head.

The first time Alec took Mabel to Red Head they climbed to the top of the mountain and looked across the sparkling water at the gleaming white houses of Baddeck, past the island with its lighthouse, to the Washabuck headland opposite and beyond up St. Patrick's Channel to the distant blue hills of Salt Mountain. As they stood gazing, Alec murmured the Gaelic words "beinn bhreagh"—beautiful mountain. From the distance came the sound of bagpipes. Alec hurried Mabel down the steep path to the shores of the Bras d'Or Lakes. He recognized the plaintive notes of a Scottish lament. Somehow it sounded strangely fitting in this beautiful far-off place and reminded him of his Scottish homeland.

Hand in hand they came in time to see the friends and neighbors of old Donald MacAulay bearing his remains to a little graveyard overlooking the lake. They followed at a respectful distance, then stood silently as MacAulay was lowered into his grave. MacAulay's twelve children—six by his first wife and six by his second—stood with heads bowed. To Mabel it seemed to be one of those moments where fate intervened, bringing the new master of Red Head to the scene at the exact moment the old master was being laid to rest.

It took seven years before the Bells' dream of owning Red Head became reality. The MacAulay farm was divided between his widow and children, and it took time to persuade them all to sell. However, Bell would not consider building until he was sure of an adequate water supply. He decided to acquire Rory MacMillan's farm, which had an excellent spring. Unfortunately, Rory couldn't make up his mind whether or not to sell, so Bell bought a hundred acres from John Matheson on one side of Rory, then two hundred and fifty acres from the widow of William MacLean on the other side of the MacMillan farm. Still Rory remained undecided. Patiently, Bell waited. Not until 1888 did Rory finally consent to sell. Once assured of an ample water supply, the Bells built a small house overlooking the harbor that could later be used as a lodge. This, together with Crescent Grove, would serve their needs until they were able to build their dream house on the point.

During that first summer at Crescent Grove with their primitive and limited accommodation, they had a few Washington friends up to visit them. But for the most part, their social life was limited to guests from the Telegraph House and local people, particularly the McCurdy family, as Mabel explained to her mother:

We have seen a great deal lately of Mr. Arthur McCurdy. He was Alec's agent in the purchase of the place and he has been over it with us and drops in constantly to play chess with Alec.[5]

There is one thing I would like very much if you could get or order for me some time in Boston and that is a set of handsome ivory chessmen. Alec wants to give it to Mr. Arthur McCurdy who has played so often with him and been so very kind. I hope I am not bothering you too much, but I am sure you would want us to show our appreciation of these people's kindness. I wish you could see old Mr. McCurdy, he is just a lovely

old man, so kindly and gentle with his grandchildren and everyone.[6]

Mrs. Dunlop from the Telegraph House one day suggested that Arthur McCurdy might be the very person Bell had been looking for as a secretary. It was unusual in such a remote village to find a well-educated man who shared Bell's enthusiasm for the telephone. McCurdy's brother William, the local member of the legislative assembly, had attended the Centennial Exhibition in Philadelphia and seen Bell's newly invented telephone. He bought three of the instruments to communicate between his home, the family store and the *Island Recorder* newspaper office. They were the first telephones in Nova Scotia. Arthur McCurdy had an inventive turn of mind as well; he invented the photographic accessory that later became the Eastman developer.

After selling the *Island Recorder*, of which he was editor in 1887, McCurdy became Bell's companion and secretary and remained with him until 1902 when he moved to Victoria, British Columbia. Bell and McCurdy planned "the Lodge" together and made a model of it. It was Mabel, however, who made sure the local carpenters carried out their plans.

When Charlie Bell came to visit they bought a steam launch so they could go exploring. They sailed around the Bras d'Or Lakes, through St. Peter's Canal and up the west coast of Cape Breton island to the village of Inverness:

It is perfectly lovely here, the archipelago of islands, and the mainland with its steep hillside sloping down to the water, makes a lovely sight. I am afraid

107

Charlie did not enjoy his tent life last night as much as he might as he and Alec were both very cold. We are now established at Squire MacDonald's house and decidedly more comfortable than we should have been in a tent this wet night. Mrs. MacDonald has lived in the "Boston States." I presume she was in service there as she has given us the best supper we have had since we came here. The first sound we heard as Mr. MacDonald showed us in was the whir of half a dozen spinning wheels! I felt transported back to the Middle Ages when we went upstairs and found the women and girls spinning wool, not as fashionable amusement but in dead earnest. We were told that they were all neighbors who in an act of neighborliness came to spin wool to make a new carpet for the dining room. Mrs. MacDonald has only been married eight months and is trying to furnish her house and the people all like the Squire so much they want to help him. He is an exceedingly nice looking man. Doesn't it seem funny to think of one being in Scotland as it were? All the people were talking Gaelic and some of them did not understand Nellie's English. Everybody here is Mac something. It is funny to see how much people here have been interested in President Garfield. I have seen pictures of him in nearly every home I have been in this summer.

I think I will go to bed now. We get up at half-past six so need to retire early. I am wondering what sort of night we are to have as I don't believe Mrs. MacDonald has more than one bed for all four of us! Decidedly we are roughing it but we are all enjoying it and are very well.[7]

We will not be here long after September comes in although if it were not for you [her mother], we should be in no hurry to leave. Are you really going to Washington in September? I don't know what Alec's plans will be, we neither of us want to look forward to leaving this lovely place only I want so much to see you my Darling Mama.[8]

During the years that Alec and Mabel lived on their beautiful mountain they called "Beinn Bhreagh," they were fortunate to have Mr. and Mrs. George Kennan, their most intimate friends, as neighbors. Kennan had been associated with Hubbard and Bell in founding the National Geographic Society. He was one of the earliest international correspondents and the author of several books on life in Russia. They visited the Bells at Crescent Grove in Baddeck. At a dinner party the following winter in the Bells' Washington home, Alec was talking enthusiastically about his recent visit to Baddeck and mentioned a little house that was for sale near Crescent Grove. On leaving the table, Kennan sent a telegram to the owner and bought the house, sight unseen. The Kennans came to Baddeck in 1889 and occupied the house now known as "Bute Arran."

Several years after Berta's death, Mabel's youngest sister Grace married her brother-in-law Charlie Bell. At first they visited the Bells in Baddeck for weeks at a time, bringing Berta's two little girls with them, but as their family grew they needed a home of their own. In 1891 they bought property near the Kennans.

Over the years Mabel's home always seemed to be filled with relatives, guests or scientific friends of Alec's.

Most of them stayed for weeks at a time. Mabel described her summer to her mother:

Although it is hard work at times, having such a large family as mine has been all summer, one misses "the old familiar faces" when they are gone. Grace says she wishes you could be here if only to enjoy Alec. He is quite a different person from what he is in Washington. Here he is the life and soul of the party. Nothing is done without him, no detail relating to our enjoyment, comfort or safety escapes him. He is forever on the go; at night when all are sleeping, he is paddling about but he is up again at his usual hour. At unusual times, when a high wind is blowing or the boats are to be moved, he is up no matter how early the hour directing and arranging everything. I think you and Papa would admire Alec very much.[9]

On the top of the mountain Alec had positioned his sheep village, complete with streets laid out with little houses for the sheep. He tried developing a strain of multi-nippled ewes that would bear several lambs instead of the usual one, all part of his interest in heredity. For Mabel this was far more fascinating than the heredity of deafness that had occupied Alec's thoughts. She explained to her mother:

Alec and I have been all over the mountain this afternoon. It is our first satisfactory walk for a long time because since his return, Alec has been spending the whole of every afternoon with the sheep in the company of the shepherds....

Alec is going to have some more land on top of the mountain brought under cultivation as it is nearly

110

level and our finest land. Then we tried to decide the most sheltered locality for the winter fold. Alec is having ten small houses built for his sheep down at the wharf and intends to have them put on wheels and dragged up the mountain grouping them in little clusters of three or four about the yard. His idea in building these small movable houses is to be able to change the fold every year, thus obviating the danger of disease which must exist when sheep spend winter after winter on the same ground and also to leave the thoroughly manured ground free for plowing and sowing.[10]

Alec was anxious that Mabel should be involved in the life of the community. He suggested that she organize a sewing class for the young women, hoping that it would develop eventually into a cottage industry. Mabel wrote:

Won't you let me know how much the work I sent you is worth? I want very much to pay the girls. I have done nothing about the sewing schools. The weather has been too bad to drive all over the country visiting the school trustees. Miss Cain is engaged and I think will bring interest and painstaking to her work. She seems to understand how to reach the people as no stranger could but she wants me to show my interest by visiting the people myself.[11]

By November Mabel was busy helping her daughter Daisy and her little friends with a theatrical wardrobe:

They acted "King Volmer and Elsie." Half our audience was composed of my sewing class and the McCurdy children and some of the farm children. They really did very well.... Alec drilled the children and especially Daisy in the elocution, working very

111

hard with them, and I felt they were getting a valuable lesson and that Daisy was willing to work far harder and was getting more training in elocution than she could any other way. Besides I wanted to give the children a treat.[12]

Years later Daisy recalled the life they led at the Lodge during that winter of 1890 when they had remained until after Christmas:

That was a wonderful winter.... I think Miss True was with us and I had lessons from her. Miss True was Mother's first teacher and she and Mother adored each other.

Father was very big. I think he weighed about 230 pounds and his thick iron-gray hair waved and curled all over his head. He hated going to a barber so his hair was generally pretty long and he always gesticulated with his head as well as his hands. He wore rough gray clothes—black and gray like his hair. I have a big woolly impression of him.

Mother was only about 32 that year—very slim in the long tight fitting dresses of the day. She had exquisite skin with a good deal of color, gray-blue eyes and masses of soft brown hair. I can see her now (almost forty years later) dressed for a walk in the snow with the little hatchet Mr. McCurdy gave her in her belt—long woolen gloves to the elbow and a close fitting sealskin cap. That she ever ploughed through the snow in a skirt to her ankles seems astonishing.

Mr. McCurdy was a very good looking man—tall and finely proportioned—with a small Van Dyke beard and long mustaches of which he was very proud.

He was Father's secretary and understudy in the everyday affairs of life. I don't think he ever helped him much in his scientific work except that he was always an interested listener—would take dictation all night long and helped make the endless little first models that Father made of every new invention he was interested in.

It was awfully cold in the house which was built for summer. I remember the struggle it was for me to say goodnight to the group around the big fire downstairs and rush upstairs through the long dark cold corridor to my room. I must confess that I usually had a little fire of my own up there but it didn't do more than take the chill off the air though it did make lovely flickering patterns on the wall that I watched as long as I could keep my eyes open. The fire shadows on the ceiling and Father's playing always come together in my memory. For almost every night after the others had all gone to bed he would sit down at the piano and play for hours and hours. He played vehemently—passionately, pouring his soul out and upstairs I would wake up at intervals and listen while watching the firelight.[13]

The month of December continued to be enjoyable, as Mabel's letter to her mother suggested:

It had just begun to snow when we left the house and the trees were quite bare, as we returned there must have been nearly two inches of snow on the evergreen trees and everything was perfectly beautiful. You will be surprised at my enthusiasm for the snow, remembering how I used to hate it, but Beinn Bhreagh snow is very different from Washington or even Cambridge snow. There it is damp and chilly, a nuisance in every way; here it is dry and crisp and nice to walk in. I used to be so cold going out in the wintertime. Here I have had several long walks when the thermometer was not very far from zero and have been as warm as toast all the time. I hope you don't think all this rhapsody is a prelude to telling you that we intend to stay here all winter! No indeed. I expect to be quite ready to go after Christmas but I am more glad all the time that we have decided to remain.[14]

A few weeks later she wrote:

We had a pleasant Christmas. It was bitterly cold, one of the coldest days we have had and I feared the children from town at all events would not come, but they all did except one poor little town girl who got left behind by mistake and the poorest child of all who was sick. We had about thirty children altogether and I think they were very much pleased with the tree and Alec's efforts for their entertainment. I know I saw my sewing girls laugh and laugh with all their might and main for the first time in my acquaintance with them. We sent to Montreal for presents so all were provided with a little gift, a cornucopia of candy and a big red apple.

We are going to light the tree again tomorrow for the workmen and their wives as one of them said he would walk miles to see such a sight and Alec is busy preparing for their entertainment.[15]

After the New Year it was time to leave Baddeck and return to Washington, as Daisy recalled:

Mr. Anderson came for us in the big sleigh with

his two beautiful gray horses—Champ and Harry—
and the thrill of it all was that the snowbanks made the
road so narrow that he had to hitch the horses tandem.
We drove around the head of the bay and then across
the ice from Baddeck to Washabuck—our way being
marked by little spruce trees set up in the snow—and as
the days were so very short, it took us three days to get to
the Strait of Canso and from there we took the train.[16]

11
Life is Not Simple

When Alec and Mabel returned to Washington after their
first visit to Baddeck in October 1885, they were aston-
ished to discover that nearly every newspaper in the country was proclaiming to the world, on the authority of the
U.S. State Department, that Bell's claim that he invented
the first telephone was false. He was being charged with
perjury and fraud. The charges were not brought in Washington where Bell lived, nor in Massachusetts where the
Bell Telephone Company, sole owner of the patents, was
domiciled, but in Tennessee. The action was instigated by
the Pan-Electric Company, a firm the courts had already
found to be infringing on Bell's patents. One of the orga-
nizers of this company and its largest shareholder was the

U.S. attorney general. For years the case dragged on, revealing corruption among high government officials. Ultimately the Pan-Electric Company died a natural death and the action was finally dropped, but not before these false charges and the attendant publicity caused the Bells a great deal of anguish. Mabel was so close to her husband that anything that caused him distress became a matter of concern to her. Several items in her journal show how they suffered:

Poor Alec, all this week he has been working hard and drawing immense drafts on the reserve of health and strength laid up this summer. He has given up everything to devote himself entirely to his letter to the Attorney General. I have scarcely spoken a dozen words to him since Sunday morning for he has dreaded to have his mind taken off the subject in hand. He has not taken a single meal with us all week.[1]

Alec said that in consequence of the cruel and unjust suit that has been brought against him, he would be unable to give his school [for the training of teachers for the deaf] the personal attention he felt was so necessary for its success and rather than have it drag on as it has been doing lately, he would put a stop to it now. After the good-byes Alec came home with a splitting headache and a heartache harder to bear. What this act and its cause has cost my husband only Dr. Radcliffe and I, who have been with him, can know.[2]

Bell, now at the height of his career, had a great many projects underway. Apart from his work on the heredity of deafness, he continued working on his inventions with his cousin Chester Bell and Sumner Tainter. He used the considerable sum of money received for the Volta Prize to establish the Volta Laboratory in Washington. Edison had already invented a machine that would record and produce sound, but the sound it produced was so jerky that his instrument was of no commercial value. However, using Edison's machine as their starting point, Bell and his associates were able to develop a much more satisfactory cylinder that produced a smooth sound. They followed their new cylinder development with the invention of the flat disc record, the form now in universal use. From his share of the proceeds after selling the invention to Edison, Bell established the Volta Bureau to increase and diffuse knowledge relating to the deaf.

In 1883 Hubbard and Bell bought a weekly magazine called *Science* from its editor John Michels. Under their direction *Science* became the official organ of the world's greatest scientific community, the American Association for the Advancement of Science. Mabel's interest was as great as Alec's in this venture. Over a period of years she contributed more than $60,000 to maintain it.

With so many projects vying for Bell's attention, it was not surprising that he had little time for the concerns of his family. Mabel had to carry these responsibilities alone. At times she complained:

I am so glad to hear that you arrived in Boston. But it was a great disappointment having you go off without spending a night with me here. There are so many things I wanted to talk over with you and Mama and Papa which it would have helped me to discuss. In that sense I do think Papa was right and that it was

selfish of you to go off. Your work will be with you as long as you live, your friends you may not have long.

I realize as I see Mama and Papa, Grace and Charlie together, how little you give me of your time and thoughts, how unwilling you are to enter into the little things, which yet make up the sum of our lives. There are so many more of those things than you realize, which I cannot decide alone. I feel as if I were giving more and more to others the dependence for help and advice that should be yours.[3]

Absorbed with bringing up her two little girls, there were times when she desperately felt the need for Alec's help:

Alec Dear, you do not realize that at no previous time did your children need their mother's and father's eye as now when their characters are developing. The little faults springing up, that if not checked, may grow serious. Elsie is about the worst companion little Daisy could have. She is so generous and careless that she gives everything up to her and even when the child is naughty, makes my work twice as hard by joining in at screaming at any punishment I feel obliged to inflict. Please come home, I want you so very much and am beginning to dread my lonely nights as I seldom escape without a fright.[4]

The passage of time didn't make the task any easier. Several years later her journal contained this entry:

The children are well. I am trying hard to awaken a love of reading in Elsie and succeeding poorly; in plain words, failing utterly. Elsie doesn't care for anything but company now. She has no resources within

118

herself and no habit of application. She is a dreadful weight on me in consequence. I feel sure that her faults are mostly due to her upbringing but how to train her into good habits now, I don't know. She is affectionate and thinks she is fond of me but I doubt it is but surface fondness and I cannot see why she would be really fond of me. It is "do this, don't do that" all the time, all day long, and I know that I oughtn't do so and at the same time I know she must be made to do something.[5]

However, by 1885, after returning from their first trip to Nova Scotia, Mabel reported: "They both have enjoyed their travels immensely and if they cannot read and scarcely write, yet they know a great deal about things that most children and many grown-ups do not know."[6]

Her concern with bringing up her children will strike a responsive chord with today's parents. However, her constant obsession with the health of her family carries a rather strident note until we reflect upon the advances made in medicine over the century. Tuberculosis and other infectious diseases took a heavy toll in almost every family, her own included. Few hospitals were available and nursing care took place at home, the duties shared by members of the family. Writing to Alec, she expressed concern for his health:

I do not think you realize how much you are to me. How much I and your children depend on you and you cannot be yourself "every inch a man" unless you have a sound mind in a sound body. Take care of your precious health and strength for the sake of your wife and helpless little ones who have only half a mother.[7]

Early one cold January morning in 1887, a police-

119

man passing 1500 Rhode Island Avenue saw flames coming from the roof of the house and quickly gave the alarm. Mabel awoke suddenly when her dog jumped excitedly onto the bed. When she realized what was happening, she had the servants dress the children warmly and take them across the street to a neighbor's home while she remained to instruct the firemen to save, above all else, her husband's library. Alec was away at the time. When the firemen tried to persuade her to leave the burning building, she pretended not to understand. Finally the smoke drove her out.

The fire was confined to the third floor, but the whole house had been drenched with water that turned quickly to ice. When Alec returned he was thankful no one had been hurt and grateful that his library had been saved, even though his study was a litter of sodden manuscripts and notebooks.

After the fire was extinguished, Mabel hired some men from a rooming house nearby to help clear away the debris and salvage whatever they could. One of the workmen, Charles Thompson, a young black from Virginia, was entrusted with cleaning up the study. Thompson did such a fine job that Mabel engaged him on the spot as a permanent member of their household staff, and for thirty-five years he served the Bell family faithfully.

Mabel refurbished their home as elegantly as it had been before the fire. Two years later they sold it to Levi P. Morton, the incoming vice-president of the United States, and for the next two years lived in a rented house on 19th Street until their new house at 1331 Connecticut Avenue was completed. This three-storey, red brick and stone residence, not quite as elaborate as the Rhode Island Avenue house, remained their Washington home for the rest of their lives.

As the American authority on the teaching of speech to the deaf, Bell was invited to London in the spring of 1888 to testify before a British royal commission on the deaf. Mabel and the children went with him. While he was in London, she joined her father and mother in Paris, and together they toured France and Spain. However, her thoughts were very much with Alec:

I certainly wish I had been there to see [you giving your testimony] although I would also have wished to be invisible. How the gentlemen must have wondered when you brought out document after document in proof of all you said. I hope you looked very neat and nice, had your hair cut and beard trimmed. I wish you would go to the best tailor in London and get yourself a swell suit and I really wish you would hire a valet temporarily. I don't think you realize even yet the importance of an irreproachable exterior although your neglect nearly cost you your wife. And say what you will, Englishmen of the class you are now addressing think more of these things than Americans.

Please be careful of yourself and don't overwork too much—I can't do without you, as I find every day. I want you with me very much and yet I don't want you to shorten your stay in London on that account. Accept all the invitations you get—and meet all the great men you can—I want to hear all about them. I always feel as if you were my second self and all the interesting people you meet I meet too and enjoy far

more than if I really met them. Never mind a little dyspepsia. We will go home to Baddeck and live on bread and milk for the rest of the summer.[8]

As Mabel realized, Alec had come to London well prepared; instead of simply testifying for a day, he was invited to continue for four days. At first he was elated, but then became discouraged. Like many husbands he vented his frustrations on his wife:

I wish you were not quite so far away. I want you so much now. I think if you were near me, you would sympathize with me but far away you cannot realize how much my heart has been wrapped up in my work and how mortified and disgusted with myself I am. I commenced so well and made a great impression but I talked too much and spoilt it all. I feel that my whole testimony whittled down to a tame conclusion.

The end is so important. I want to get the proof [of my testimony] especially as the Chairman gave me liberty to append to the evidence a brief statement recapitulating the chief points. That will be my chance to end properly. I am as nervous as can be over it. I have worked so hard over the whole matter, you know I have, and I don't want to end in failure. I feel quite ill over the whole matter, and sick at heart, and I have no one to whom I can turn. You haven't a particle of sympathy for my work [with the deaf]...there I am fated ever to be alone. If you were only here, you would have sympathy for me—I am so miserable and unhappy alone.[9]

Although the Bells were financially secure enough to live lavishly and travel abroad a great deal, Mabel was

122

always concerned about their expenses. It was difficult for them to live within their income. They were always waiting for the next quarterly dividend in order to meet their commitments. Mabel frequently wrote letters such as this:

I have just sent off my check to Charlie but won't you please be as careful as you can, it is just the small bills that make up the big total and I have some very large bills to pay and no money to do it with.[10]

A letter of Alec's explains one of the reasons Mabel had such difficulty managing their finances in spite of her attempts to economize:

So you want your husband just to "loan" you some money in a "business way" to enable you to live while I am away. You poor little Mabel—is anything more wanted to prove what a selfish heartless fellow I am—to let you go on in this way as I do without helping you. I regret the day we handed over our business matters to Charlie. Before that we managed nicely together and I knew exactly how our investments stood and all about them—now I know next to nothing and leave them all to you to manage alone....

I think it is quite proper that the Laboratory should be supported out of Laboratory profits—and *Science* to be aided out of the same fund, and if you like, I will sell some of my inventor's shares for that purpose. It is not fair to you that *Science* should eat a big hole out of your income every year—and that your income should be cut down still more by large investments of capital that bring no present return. I think there are few wives as self-sacrificing as you are—very few that would allow their husbands to take thousands

of dollars from their income—to invest in unprofitable enterprises like *Science*.[11]

Apart from her concern about their finances, Mabel was worried about Elsie's health after she suffered an attack of convulsions early in 1884. Although the attack did not recur, Elsie grew increasingly nervous and within the next few years developed a severe case of chorea, more commonly known as St. Vitus' dance. Alec felt confident that Swedish exercise and fresh air would soon cure her, but her condition worsened and Mabel insisted that they consult the noted neurologist Dr. S. Weir Mitchell, inventor of the "rest cure." He advised that Elsie be taken from her parents and their eventful household for a time. For over a year she lived in Philadelphia with a nurse-companion who carried out the treatments Dr. Mitchell recommended. The doctor thought her well enough to spend the summer of 1890 in Baddeck, but the excitement of family life became too much for her, and instead of getting better she grew steadily worse. Mabel explained in letters to her mother:

Poor little Elsie, we had to send her back to Philadelphia. I do not know how deeply she feels the leaving of Beinn Bhreagh and us all. She told the doctor that she knew she wasn't getting better and she was becoming discouraged. She got off very nicely; we rowed her over smooth glassy seas, and after rowing about for a little over an hour, we made fast to the off side of the S.S. *Marion* and got her on board almost unperceived. In her stateroom saying good-bye she was very excited and more uncontrolled than I ever saw her before, but still she seemed to have no *mauvais*

honte and was extremely anxious to go on deck among the people.[12]

How good you always are to your children and grandchildren. It is so hard for you to have to go off to Philadelphia and yet it is a great comfort to me to know you will be there and the greatest help to Alec. Won't you let me know what the doctor says about my poor little girl? I do not feel that Alec tells me just what the doctor says. He means to of course, but I think his account is often colored by his own feelings. Besides it will be several days before I get Alec's version and then his memory will have lost its freshness.[13]

Some months later Alec wanted to take Elsie to Washington to see his mother, but Mabel took a very firm stand against it:

Please don't take Elsie to Washington with you. I am willing to take more risks with my children for your mother than for anyone else because they are her only grandchildren but think how long it has taken Elsie to get as well as she is, a whole year and four months, and how dreadful it would be for her to have a relapse now. Your mother would not thank you for making her the cause of such a disaster. You think Elsie perfectly well again. She certainly is well but she is not established in her good health. If it were anything else, I would not say a word against you taking her but think of having to pay for it with another year's separation from our child.[14]

By the end of 1891 Elsie was greatly improved in health. Mabel was anxious that her daughters have the advantage of education and travel abroad enjoyed by so many well-to-do American families of the period. Alec wouldn't leave his own work at the time so Mabel set off without him, accompanied by the faithful Charles Thompson. It was not easy for her to travel alone, but she showed great strength in coping with the situation. She wrote from the ship:

The children are really very good and thoughtful. Daisy is a nice little one to translate between me and the Captain and to keep me informed as well as she can of what is being said at the table. Elsie is a great relief and manages far better than I dared hope.[15]

Bell's work absorbed him completely. His sense of urgency increased with each passing year so that he resented any distractions. When Mabel was with him, she shared his work, never minding if he woke her in the middle of the night to explain some new idea. When they were separated, she suffered a sense of isolation:

Your telegrams never say anything of yourself, how you are and what you are doing. I can't stand this silence much longer—I must have a letter no matter how busy you are. Have you really no desire to make me share in your thoughts and feelings? I begin to feel dreadfully hurt.

I wonder if you will take the trouble to read all this. I wonder do you ever think of me in the midst of that work of yours of which I am so proud and yet so jealous, for I know it has stolen from me a part of my husband's heart, for where his thoughts and interests lie, there too must his heart be. I live in hope that you will not quite forget me and that we may pass many another summer like the last [at Beinn Bhreagh] when we had thoughts and interests in common.[16]

In spite of Alec's great obsession with his work, to the exclusion of everything else, he did sense Mabel's unhappiness:

There is a great fear, my Darling, rising in my heart, and I am so restless and nervous that I do not know what to do. Quite apart from your health—I am afraid of a distance between us—for something tells me that you care less for me—and about me—when I am far away. My letters do not please you—and yours sometimes hurt me too. Do not let us be separated any longer than can be helped—for when we are together suspicions fly away—and we are happy.

Oh Mabel Dear, I love you more than you can ever know. I feel I have neglected you; deaf-mutes, gravitation and any other hobby has been too apt to take the first place in my thoughts. Yet, all the time my heart was yours alone. I will throw everything to one side and this summer shall be devoted to you and the children.

You have grown into my heart my darling and taken root there—and you cannot be plucked out without tearing it to pieces.[17]

12
Life at Beinn Bhreagh

WHEN ALEC AND MABEL BELL first acquired property in Baddeck, they intended it simply as a summer retreat. As they purchased more and more land, their retreat developed into a large estate employing many local people. Mabel threw her heart and soul into this enterprise; whether traveling abroad or living in Washington, thoughts concerning Beinn Bhreagh remained very much in her mind. Alec wanted to be there in early spring when the new lambs were born. Although Mabel felt she must stay in Washington with the children, her letters are full of her interest in all that was happening at Baddeck:

My thoughts are constantly with you at Beinn Bhreagh. I am sure the sheep are safe in your care but there are so many other things in which I am equally interested; the warehouse, the roads and the workmen's cottages. Why cannot the gardener's cottage go up at the Point? I am most anxious to get the gardens there started as soon as possible. It will only take eighteen months, or at the most two years, to build the house but five years is all too short an allowance for gardens to grow to real beauty and they will not be begun until the gardener is close at hand.

Here is the order of importance in my mind: 1. Roads, 2. Warehouse, 3. Gardener's cottage, 4. Mr. Ellis's cottage, 5. Workmen's cottages, 6. House at the Point. I say roads first because I want them this sum-

mer, not wide ones but good narrow ones over which a good strong pony in a cart can go. Then comes the warehouse; Mr. Ellis's cottage does not seem immediately imperative if those two other cottages can be obtained temporarily. However, we must provide decent places for our workmen before we build a big house for ourselves.[1]

In 1891, while still in Washington, Mabel was taken to the home of Senator Eugene Hale. On that particular day Mrs. Hale had gathered a small group of women who had been meeting once a week for a number of years to discuss things of mutual interest. These women were all eminent in political, army, navy, artistic and literary circles at the time. They came together to discuss current events, books and pictures and various projects that interested them. Their informal meetings had come to mean so much to these ladies that on that day they decided to form themselves into a regular organization, which was to become the "Washington Club."

The discussion was followed with great interest by Mabel, whose gaze never left the lips of the speaker. Her mind seethed with an idea. It seemed to her that if these women at the heart of things in Washington, with all the resources of information and entertainment at hand, felt the need to come together and discuss things, how much greater must be the need—and how much greater would be the benefit—for those women in far-off Baddeck, so dependent on their own resources.

When she got back to Beinn Bhreagh she discussed her idea with Alec, Mr. McCurdy and McCurdy's sister Georgina; they were all enthusiastic. Alec had been concerned that Mabel might be lonely at Beinn Bhreagh after their summer visitors left unless she made friends among the people of Baddeck. If Mabel could organize a ladies club, it would give her the friends she needed and do a great deal for the women of Baddeck. The village's social life was fragmented by religion and politics. The few Roman Catholics had little social contact with the rest of the community, while the wives of the staunch Conservatives hardly dared associate socially with those women whose husbands were Liberals. Both McCurdys recommended that Mabel select her friends regardless of such social barriers. Having decided that the club's purpose was to acquire general knowledge and provide sociability, the McCurdys offered to provide her with the names of women they thought would be most interested in such a club.

They held the first meeting at the Lodge on October 10, 1891. Mabel sent the gig, a long row boat that required three men to row, and brought those ladies whom she invited to form the new club from across the bay. She longed to call the club simply "The Baddeck Club," but hesitated to suggest it lest their men object to women taking possession of the village name, so instead it was called "The Young Ladies Club of Baddeck." On its thirteenth anniversary, shortly after Bell's death, the ladies decided to change the name. Many of the older founding members were still active and the original name no longer seemed appropriate. They changed it to "The Alexander Graham Bell Club," and it continued to meet regularly to this day during the winter months; it is possibly the oldest continuing ladies club in Canada and has done more than anything else to keep the memory of Mabel Bell alive in that community.

Not only did the club provide Mabel with life-long friends, it also gave her the confidence to overcome her handicap by speaking in public. Mabel shared with Elsie her pleasure in her new-found friends:

Yesterday was lovely. The Ladies' Club Board came over for a meeting at four o'clock. We talked until five-thirty and then got out our needlework or knitting and gossiped until six, had a jolly dinner and then Papa showed us lantern slides until John came home at eight-thirty with the mail and our guests departed and we felt we had a beautiful long evening. I tell you what, there is nothing like real country life [as here in Baddeck] when you know how to manage it so that you have real sociability. I have more of this here than I do in Washington.[2]

Bell was invited to give a talk to the club on the parents association that he had been instrumental in forming in connection with the schools for the deaf in the United States. As a result, and encouraged by Mabel, in 1895 many of the parents of those attending the Baddeck Academy organized themselves into a similar association. From this small beginning grew the Canadian Home and School Association, which now has branches in almost every town and village throughout the country.

When George Kennan suggested Baddeck should have its own public library, he found in Mabel Bell an enthusiastic supporter. She not only contributed generously to the purchase of books, but for many years provided the community with a disused church, which she renovated and called Gertrude Hall, as a place to house their library.

An important annual event at Beinn Bhreagh was

the Harvest Home Celebrations, which Mabel's cousin Mary Blatchford attended and of which she left this description:

The invitations were sent out on Monday to all the men who had been employed on the estate this year, to come at two o'clock with their families for games and dancing. There were about fifty men included in the invitation and their "families" on this occasion were elastic and took in most of the population within a radius of twenty miles.

Great preparations were made for receiving our guests and the day was brilliant although rather windy. After breakfast Mr. McCurdy rowed Mabel and me to Baddeck, about two miles away, to choose the prizes. At the little shop in Baddeck we had the undivided attention of all hands, including the customers who stood solemnly about in rapt observation. At the last Harvest Home everybody had a prize but Mabel thought it would be a little more exciting, if such a word could be applied to this solid race, if only ninety percent came in for prizes. We chose neckties, suspenders, scarfs, hammers, knives, etc., and came home laden.

At two o'clock the people began to file up to the tennis ground, a lovely spot on the mountain slope, and there in time we followed them. I wish you could have seen Mabel, Grace and the children. They were such pictures as one seldom sees outside of European galleries. Mabel so fair and madonna-like, with Grace's baby in her arms, Grace with her exquisite piquant face that changes every minute, Elsie and Daisy tall and dark as Gypsies, with magnificent eyes.

The games opened with walking on stilts followed by the throwing of the hammer, putting the shot, potato race, running, etc. Afterward we walked to the "warehouse," why so called I cannot imagine—I should call it an immense two-storey barn. On the ground floor were tables laden with sandwiches of every description and more pies and cakes than I have ever seen. Boilers full of tea and coffee were steaming on the stove and barrels of gingerale were on tap. The barn was trimmed with vegetables and flowers and was a delight to see. Mrs. Kennan and I sat on the phaeton which was warehoused in one corner. Mabel was mounted on the groom's seat behind and there we were served with things to eat and drink. When even the boys could eat no more—and they were all as solemn about their eating as if they were going to be hanged as soon as they were done—we all went up to the loft which had been cleared for dancing.

A fiddler was on hand and fiddled steadily. The dancing began at once with four couples who went through what I would call a grand mixture of quadrille, lancers, double-shuffle and jig. It was the thing I longed for years to see and was worth the journey here and back.

Mrs. Kennan, with the courage of her sex, added to that caught from her wonderful husband, accepted an invitation to open the dance with a great clumsy-looking boy whose shoes alone must have weighed a ton. But, dear me, how he did trip it. His feet went so fast I should not have known whether he had shoes on or not. He shuffled and kicked and pranced and

133

twirled, now and then snatching Mrs. Kennan around the waist and spinning her around in bewildering mazes, then dropping her suddenly, while she smiled and looked pretty as if she knew all about it and with wonderful agility got out of the way of the other couples.

One old woman, dancing with a boy young enough to be her grandson, interested me specially. She moved nothing but her feet but they went like lightning. Her face was set like flint, her hands hung straight down and she danced as if her life were at stake. It all seemed more like some religious ritual than something done for amusement. At intervals one of the men would snap his fingers or crash down with one heel but always with the same solemnity, not a smile on a single face or a word exchanged at any time.

This dance was called the "Scottish Eights" and was followed by the "Scottish Fours" and the "Scottish Twos." My old woman wiped her face and went in for every dance. When I thanked her, she did not understand a word as she spoke only Gaelic. A man at her side answered for her, "Oh, she's all right," from which I gathered he didn't understand much more than she. After a time the loft got very hot and Gardiner took me home but I felt that my old woman was still at it, with her set face and hanging arms like a dancing doll worked by strings.[3]

The house on the point was finally completed in November 1893 and called Beinn Bhreagh Hall. It remains today much as Mabel created it, a period piece typical of many of the houses built by wealthy Americans in Newport, Rhode Island, during the nineteenth century. A large and sprawling wooden house, brown with white trim, a sunporch and a number of towers and verandas, surrounded by beautiful lawns and gardens and a magnificent view of the Bras d'Or Lakes, it is an imposing sight set on the side of its own private mountain. Mabel was always keenly interested in her home and over the years added treasures collected on their travels from all over the world.

Mary Blatchford came for a second visit in 1911 and described Beinn Bhreagh Hall:

The new house of Mr. Bell's is a mile and a half from the old one of twenty years ago—the Lodge—but not so high up on the mountain as I had thought—quite on the water in fact. As we drove up the avenue from the wharf and came in sight of the house, I saw that it was illuminated with colored lights; for me, as Mr. Bell was careful to explain. Alternate globes of red and yellow ran up the pillars of the porch and it was so very pretty. But the prettiest thing of all was Mabel herself. Everything here begins with her and works round again to the same. The grandchildren—three in the house and five more down at the "Lodge"—call her Grammy....

I don't know where to begin in telling you of this house. As I am sitting in my own room, I will begin with that. When Mabel brought me in, it was brilliantly lighted; the first thing that caught my eye was the frieze. The pattern was in relief and furthermore it was made of mussel shells, embedded in white plaster, and all in a very regular charming design. There are two thousand and seven shells, for I counted them, all

gathered here by women. The work was carried on under difficulties because the designers worked faster than the gatherers. The shells are carefully chosen with regard to size in shaping the figures, and the delicate color of the inside of the shells make a charming decoration. The rest of the wall is cream colored and the woodwork is of some light brown wood of varied shading.

The floor is nearly covered with four rugs. Two of them Pekin and two of light gray fur—Chinese dogs, heads, tails and feet included—one before the fireplace and one before the dressing table. The couch is covered with an immense embroidered cotton rug that sweeps the floor, which was bought in Lucknow, probably made in Cashmere. The ground color is white and the decorations are in red and black with dashes of green—very gorgeous. On the foot of the couch is a fur rug from Japan. Twelve little bright brown beasts with their noses side by side and two little feet straight out behind make one row; behind them is a second row without heads, then more rows, five in all, making sixty little Japanese beasts for one rug, lined with brown broadcloth—all very lovely and warm. But alas for the little beasts. On the bed—for I have one bed indoors and one bed out-of-doors—is another rug of skins of eider ducks; skins on both sides with green and white heads on one side. It is very delicate and the soft brown fur comes off at the touch; I should never dare to use it, or wish to, but Mabel says she has had it for a long time.

The dressing table is more like an altar than anything else. It is eighteen inches wide and six feet long and breast high covered with an Indian drapery falling to the ground, and a Japanese scarf of drawn work laid over the top; the two tall antique brass candlesticks and two statuettes and a quaint hanging lamp or holy water bowl hanging on one side.

The French window or glass door opening on the sleeping porch is hung with Indian curtains, and the other opening on the hall is hung with a Norwegian curtain. I asked Mabel if there was anything in the house that came from Jordan and Marsh, and she said, "Not one single thing." There is an open fireplace in the room with stacks of wood brought up every morning. The sleeping porch is protected by canvas which can be drawn at will; the bed itself is against the stone chimney of my room, and all the rest is view. Sky above, water below, and Baddeck and Washabuck circling round, full south.[4]

It was an ideal home for entertaining, and during summer it was filled to overflowing with friends and relatives who came for weeks at a time. Mabel's Baddeck friends were always included in parties given to honor these guests.

Royal visitors were entertained at Beinn Bhreagh Hall on a number of occasions. Mabel wrote to Daisy in October 1897 giving an account of the visit of the governor general of Canada and his wife, Lord and Lady Aberdeen:

Well my Darling, the Aberdeens have come and gone and now I will tell you all about them. It was the greatest shame though that it was pouring hard all the time they were here and so spoilt the effect of the hard work the townspeople bestowed on decorating Baddeck.

The table was pulled out to its uttermost length, still another leaf improvised with one and a half of another table, thus making room for thirty people to sit at. I got immense quantities of hydrangea, marigolds and sweet peas but time was getting on and I knew I should never get done by one o'clock, so Mrs. Kennan came over and helped. I was so sorry to miss the reception in Baddeck but it was impossible and the rain made it disagreeable anyway. After it was over, the party came over here. By this time it was after two and lunch had been set for one, so we were more than ready. Papa went in town but Elsie and I awaited them here. They came in the buckboard, Lord and Lady Aberdeen, Lady Marjorie their daughter, Lt. Keane, R.N., the Aide-de-camp and Papa. Wasn't it pouring, the road ran rivers of mud but fortunately the party did not seem to mind the rain or be wet, unless Lord Aberdeen was. I had Georgina [a maid] waiting on the landing going upstairs and Rose at the head and I thought that was enough, but evidently "Her Excellency" didn't think so, for she waited for me to go up with her which I obediently did.... Lady Marjorie was the only one of the party I could really understand or was understood by. She did not have much to say but was not shy and took off her things as if used to looking after herself and other people too.

Downstairs the rest of the party began to assemble. Lord Aberdeen is a slight man, not as tall or as big as his wife and about the most nervous human being I ever saw in my life except Elsie at her worst. He was not still a moment, constantly moving and talking incessantly. There was some delay about getting the guests paired and meanwhile Lady Aberdeen sat in my big rocking chair and the people stood round the room looked as stately and pretty as possible with a big fire in the great fireplace....

At last Papa led Lady Aberdeen in. Lord Aberdeen gave me his arm and followed and he immediately seated himself in his place without waiting for me or anyone else. It seemed a rather queer position to be standing there, the gentleman seated at the table and already busily engaged looking at his dinner card, while my company was perplexedly straggling in trying to find their places at the long table. I finally decided that if my gentleman sat, I would too, and there were Papa and Lady Aberdeen at one side and Lord Aberdeen and I at the other chatting away as well as we could while the rest looked after themselves.

Mrs. Kennan came in with Premier Murray [of Nova Scotia] and sat on Lord Aberdeen's other hand, fortunately for me, because I could do absolutely nothing with him. Mrs. Kennan had all she could do to attend to him and finally had to fairly turn her back on her next neighbor and almost stop eating. He talked at a railroad speed and asked questions without number about all the people at the table. He remembered the names of all he had seen before and he wanted to know who each one was and all about them. He talked to me and Mrs. Kennan indiscriminately and whenever she tried to repeat to me what he had said, he talked across to Papa and wobbled about in his chair so that Mrs. Kennan could not speak to me either before or behind him.

Premier Murray who sat on my right was almost as difficult to tackle in a different way. He had nothing whatever to say for himself. If he understood me well and good, his face would light up and he would answer, then relapse into stony silence. If he did not understand, he might glance at me, more often he simply looked straight before him but never at such times would a muscle of his face relax. It was like trying to get life out of a stone image and oh, wasn't I tired. But this was only my experience. Across the table Papa and Lady Aberdeen and Miss McCurdy seemed to be having a very good time and old Mr. McCurdy and Mrs. Howell were quite brilliant, Lady Aberdeen joining occasionally. Elsie found the Aide-de-camp rather heavy weather in spite of his gold lace, but still they got on very well.

The lunch was really beautiful and Mrs. Kennan and both "Excellencies" enjoyed it immensely but unfortunately it was half-past two before we sat down and we were due at Gertrude Hall at three. Miss McCurdy had already told the club members that we would not be there before 3:30, but as the lunch progressed, it became evident that we wouldn't be there anywhere near the time, and Lord Aberdeen got more fidgety than ever. Miss McCurdy and Mrs. Kennan assured him that the people would not mind, in fact all the Club Officers were right here and Mrs. Kennan saw his wife elevate her eye-brows to him in a peculiar way so he quieted down until after the ducks were served. Then Lady Aberdeen's eyes moved again and Lord Aberdeen immediately became anxious and finally begged to be excused as he wanted to speak to Lady Aberdeen. Then he got up as suddenly as he sat down and I got up too, so the whole party came out and left lunch three-quarters through.

It was arranged that the ladies were to go into town and he and his suite would remain with Papa and we would come back for afternoon tea. This we did.

I presided at Gertrude Hall, welcomed Lady Aberdeen, and Miss McCurdy as President spoke a few words, then Lady Aberdeen spoke for half an hour. Coming home, still in the rain, we found Papa, Mr. Kennan, Mr. McCurdy had been having a lovely time with Lord Aberdeen. Papa and Lord Aberdeen talked flying machines and sheep and Lord Aberdeen afterwards showed me that he was carrying away a souvenir, Papa's pencil diagrams. He seemed particularly pleased with Mr. McCurdy and called him to help him tell me some stories. Finally, and I think regretfully, they left, Papa escorting them to the steamer.[5]

Against this background of family and social life at Beinn Bhreagh there was always Bell's work. All his life he had been fascinated by the possibility of flight, but it was not until he was established at Beinn Bhreagh that he came to devote the greater part of his time and attention to the subject. As early as 1894, Professor S.P. Langley of the Smithsonian Institution visited Beinn Bhreagh and witnessed some of Bell's experiments. Two years later Langley reciprocated by inviting Bell to Quantico, Virginia, to witness a trial of his own large-sized model of a flying machine.

Mabel was very interested in Alec's experiments

with the theory of flight. Although many people, including Lord Kelvin, were skeptical of the value of his work, Mabel believed in it. Lord Kelvin wrote Mabel:

When I spoke to him [Bell] on the subject at Halifax, I wished to dissuade him from giving his valuable time and resources to attempts which I believed, and still believe, could only lead to disappointment, if carried out with any expectation of leading to a useful flying machine.[6]

Mabel followed her husband's experiments so closely that she was able to write:

I think I understand your experiments even if I don't know the higher mathematics. I think I could explain how you worked out that curve if you let me alone long enough to digest it in my own way. At least I believe thoroughly in you Alec Dear.[7]

I am very much interested indeed in your flying machines. At last you have come up with something I can understand.[8]

Many of Bell's attempts to fly his models met with failure, but he never lost faith:

Although numerous attempts to fly have been attended with only indifferent success on account of a leaky boiler [in the engine he was using], I have the feeling that this machine may possibly be the father of a long line of vigorous descendants that will plough the air from Beinn Bhreagh to Washington—and perhaps revolutionize the world. Who can tell? Think of the telephone![9]

13
Their Daughters' Romances

AS THEIR DAUGHTERS MATURED, both Mabel and Alec were concerned that Elsie and Daisy should receive the kind of education that would prepare them to take their places in the social life of Washington. Alec considered that fluent French was an education. He suggested that Mabel place them with a socially prominent family in Paris where in addition to learning the language they would become acquainted with French people.

Mabel dreaded the prospect of traveling alone with her teenaged daughters, even though accompanied by the faithful Charles Thompson. However, she sympathized with Alec's desire to remain at Beinn Bhreagh to pursue his flying machine experiments, and her daughters' welfare was so important that she agreed to set off for Europe in the spring of 1895 without him. He promised to join them later in the summer.

Mabel wrote Alec shortly after their arrival:

The children have been very good and done all I asked of them. Elsie has looked very handsome and talked right and left in broken French, Italian and English with an ease and composure of manner that amazes me. After all, I don't think she will be a wallflower. Daisy is quieter but she is a dear, thoughtful child and seems to have more heart than I gave her

credit for. I am beginning to think of the advisability of putting the children into the Convent of the Sacred Heart for a month. This Convent is full of French girls, none of whom are less than noble. Among girls of their own age, the children would learn French much more quickly than among grown people. My idea now is to keep the children in Paris for a month and let them explore the city and learn its history. Then take them somewhere else when it grows too hot. They could have music and singing lessons better here than anywhere else. I don't think a short stay as boarders at the Convent would do them any harm; and I am sure would be best for the acquirement of French.

I like being with my children after those years of absence and I do not feel that the absence has separated them from me. If only I might dare to expect letters from you often, much of the loneliness of exile would be gone. I wish I knew where you were today— Washington or Beinn Bhreagh?[1]

In this letter to her husband she mused on the character of each daughter:

I do not think it can be usual to meet such a transparent nature as Elsie's. She is so thoroughly frank and unreserved that you see the best and worst of her at once. All her hardness, selfishness and want of sympathy, her absorption in herself and her pleasure in her own good looks, and at the same time, her perfect sincerity and honesty, her great desire to do right, to be a good woman and conquer her faults. She never sulks and is wonderfully obedient. Daisy is far more reserved and ready to argue a point of obedience but very thoughtful with a mind so bright and clear and resourceful that it is a delight to watch her meeting any little difficulty. Elsie does all the talking in French. She is less shy about stumbling along than Daisy whose language I believe is more correct.[2]

Alec sent Mabel a copy of his letter to Professor Langley thanking him for the opportunity to watch the trial of his large model of a flying machine at Quantico, Virginia. Mabel responded with encouragement:

I think you wrote a handsome note to Professor Langley and I am glad his flying machine works. How does this affect you? Will you have to stop experimenting or do you think Professor Langley has left something for you to achieve? I don't want you to give up. It was for that that I was willing to come over alone instead of insisting that you come with us.[3]

After living in Paris for almost a month she was able to write Alec:

I am glad to say the conviction never wavers that as far as my children's welfare is concerned I did right to come. If I doubted that, I should be horribly homesick.

I took the children to the Louvre this morning and we spent an hour among the naked statues. Both were vastly edified thereby and somewhat to my horror improved their knowledge of natural history on a point at which it had hitherto been deficient. It seems to me there used to be fig leaves about and there are none any more. I don't think their absence an improvement.[4]

Although Alec hadn't wanted to leave his own

work and go to Europe, after a month's absence from his family he got lonely and suggested coming over earlier than planned. But Mabel took a firm stand:

Leave them here quietly for another month or two and then come and take them and show them the wonders of Switzerland. They will come closer to you than ever before and you will help them as you could in no other way. If you come now, it would be a great delight to have you with us but as far as the children learning French is concerned, we might as well go back to Baddeck if you were with us. The only thing to do would be for you and me to go off traveling and leave the children here alone, which would be a melancholy thing all around. On the other hand, it is dreadfully hard to have you all alone at Beinn Bhreagh and be away for so long. But if we are in earnest in the object for which we crossed the ocean, I can't see anything for it but to continue as we are.

If you come later, we will have such a good time together that it will pay for our temporary separation now. You will not be harassed with the feeling that you have run away from the Annual Convention [of the Teachers of the Deaf] and I will not feel that I have needlessly interfered with your flying machine experiments. Please remember that I am more interested in them than anything you have done for years and I would feel half my joy in our reunion spoilt if you left them.[5]

She continued to keep Alec informed of their plans:

Mrs. Mauro [an American friend] is going to Brabayon with me to see if we can find a French family there for the children when we leave here. I would like

146

them to have some time alone with French people as you wished. I think they will do better next month than they would have done at first and will be less homesick.

They are still children, obedient to my will, yet old enough to have opinions of their own and individuality enough to be interesting. They never again will be in the condition they now are, willing to submit themselves unreservedly to my judgment and desiring no other companionship. By and by they will think their own way as good as mine and other companionship more pleasant. Therefore, they will never again be so absolutely our own. While they are in this state, still obedient children, but intelligent, appreciative women, I want you to be with them. I would like them to have a month in a French family and then a month traveling with you.[6]

Mabel enjoyed her children very much on this trip but did have moments of discouragement, which she shared with Alec:

Sometimes it seems as if the children aren't gaining enough to make it worthwhile our coming abroad. Elsie is so heavy and lazy sometimes, she wants everything with no trouble—it is very discouraging. Daisy works much better. Excuse me—one must have periods of ups and downs and I am tired this morning. Probably I shall think everything is splendid tomorrow. But it is hard trying to do the best for one's children.[7]

Alec arrived in Paris in mid-August. They went first to the Channel Islands and then traveled about Switzerland, returning to Washington in the autumn and bringing with them happy memories of a glorious summer—particularly of that last month when the girls had their father's undivided attention. Upon their return home the girls were enrolled in a boarding school. It was to be the last of Elsie's schooling because the following year she was to make her debut in Washington society. Much as Mabel longed to spend early spring at Beinn Bhreagh with Alec, she felt she could remain in Washington and cultivate her friends and acquaintances. She wrote Alec:

I do realize that our children have not had the opportunities that most other girls of their position have. They suffer from having a deaf mother and a father so absorbed in his work that he won't go out and make friends for them.[8]

She made a real effort to extend her social life beyond their family circle by going out into society and entertaining in her own home. Mrs. Kennan did a great deal to encourage her:

I have three invitations for Thursday, to dinner, to a musical and to the National Geographic Society's reception. On Friday comes my little evening party for Mr. and Mrs. Kennan. On Saturday I go to a luncheon party. I was never invited to two luncheon parties before in my life so I feel a bit encouraged. But still, I do wish I were a little less lazy and more worthy to be your wife.

Well, I did have the best time I ever had at a big party [Geographic Society's reception]. I went alone except for Miss Tisdale whom I chaperoned, and Papa of course [the president of the Geographic Society] was too busy to look after me but from the first moment until the last I was not left alone a minute.

Before the reception I dined at Mrs. Brown's and had a very good time indeed. Mr. Kennan was on

one side and somebody else unknown on the other and both were very nice. Mrs. Kennan sat opposite and as usual was ready to help me out of any difficulty and start me off again. She is always so good to me that way, she seems to have me as much on her mind as my own mother would have.[9]

In 1895 Mabel wrote a fascinating article for the Annual Convention of the Teachers of the Deaf entitled "The Subtle Art of Speech Reading" in which she explained how she was able to lip read. Her article was later published in the Atlantic Monthly and translated into a number of foreign languages. She explained to Alec:

Mrs. Kennan says she has heard it [the article] referred to even this winter and she thinks it has helped me a great deal with people as they know better how to talk to me. Also, she says people have told her that they understand me and thought I understood them much better this winter. I think it is true, I have pushed more this year than ever before and my experiences in Baddeck [particularly the Ladies' Club] have given me more courage.

Mrs. Kennan said Papa told her that I entertained better than anyone in Washington. Don't think I am getting vain, but I would like to feel that I am not altogether a drawback to you.[10]

Although her Washington social life gave Mabel satisfaction, she worried about the cost of maintaining two expensive establishments. She wrote frequently to Mr. McCurdy urging him to curtail expenses at Beinn Bhreagh, and she confided to Alec in a letter written in 1896:

Mr. McCurdy says that he has had but one letter

from me that hasn't contained a scolding for someone; he thinks Washington can't agree with me. I think living away from you doesn't. I always get dreadfully worried about money matters and everything seems to come down on me alone. At home at Beinn Bhreagh there is always you and Mr. McCurdy to help me. Here I have to go through all the business alone.[11]

At least she had the satisfaction of knowing that her efforts at entertaining in the spring brought their reward the following winter. Alec was still at Beinn Bhreagh:

Debutantes' tea and reception cards are beginning to come in thick and fast. Our party for Elsie's debut has been announced in all the papers several times. It is to be on December 7, 1896, and you must come in plenty of time. Over 550 invitations have been sent out. I am not as much alarmed as I would be if Charles did not assure me that we have had 500 people in the 19th Street house [a smaller house]. The people are nearly all people whose names have always been on my list and would think themselves slighted if not invited to meet your daughter.[12]

As Daisy was away at boarding school, Mabel gave her an account of the preparations for Elsie's party:

For the reception I am going to have the musicians in the curve of the hall thus taking up very little room. Supper will be served in the dining room until eleven, then the doors will be shut and the tables cleared and the room made ready for dancing. I wish you were going to be here to see it—it does not seem right that Elsie should have her first coming-out party without you.[13]

150

A few weeks later, after the party was over, she wrote to Daisy again:

The party seems to have been a success. Elsie looked very pretty indeed. She had good color and carried herself well. The poor child confessed afterwards that she had not slept much the night before thinking that she would not get as many flowers as other debutantes but she got quite a lot. There was one big bouquet of American beauties and lilies of the valley from Papa which she carried. Another of pink roses from Grandmama. Pink carnations from Uncle Charlie; he really gave her the American beauties but exchanged with Papa as the carnations were all Papa could get and were not as becoming. Grandmama arranged the flowers in the parlor herself. There were at least 450 people in attendance. Dancing began about twelve and continued until two. Elsie was very pleased to be asked for the cotillion at the Bachelor's Ball.[14]

After her debut, Elsie enjoyed the attention of a number of admirers. Mabel was most concerned lest she become emotionally involved with someone who would not make a suitable husband. She wrote anxiously to Alec: "Please be careful of your health. I never needed you more than I do now. I feel so worried about our children's future. I want you at hand."[15]

Mabel's fears were unwarranted. Elsie thoroughly enjoyed the attention she received from her admirers, but she was not ready to take any of them seriously:

Gilbert Grosvenor is here quite often enough and what is worse, Elsie monopolizes him all the time. I like Gilbert and so far as I am concerned, she can do

151

as she likes about him, but of course he can't marry for years. Our own experience was surely sufficiently hard to make us unwilling to have Elsie subject to a similar experience.[16]

Gilbert Grosvenor was the son of Bell's friend, Professor Edwin A. Grosvenor, for many years a professor at Robert College, Constantinople, where Gilbert had been born in 1875. Dr. Grosvenor returned to America and occupied the chair of modern government and international law at Amherst College, from which institution his twin sons, Gilbert and Edwin, graduated in 1897 at the top of their class. After leaving Amherst College, Gilbert taught French, German and public speaking at a school in New Jersey and was engaged in a special study of French and English literature.

Mabel's ambitions for her daughters were not only social, as she explained in this letter to Elsie:

I am ambitious for you both in every way, I want you to have a broad outlook on life, to know not only the life of your family circle and equals but the life of other people, of the poor, of the army and navy, of students, of thinkers, of socialists as well as philosophers.[17]

In 1898 Bell took his family to Japan where the emperor received him. Mabel observed that this exposure to an entirely different culture was of great value to her daughters, who nicknamed their father Daddysan as a result of the visit. Yet she remained very concerned that their family circle contained few eligible young men, and was anxious that Alec should take the girls to Europe and have them meet other young men before Elsie drifted into a permanent relationship with Gilbert Grosvenor. When she suggested this to Alec, he objected strenuously:

I am anxious that my work should live after I am gone—but I cannot go on with it if interrupted constantly by change of residence.... I feel that the importance of my work is sufficient to demand some consideration and that it is not right to compel me to lay it all down again this year after the middle of June for the sake of a trip to Europe.

My children have the greater part of their lives before them—mine is behind me. I am not willing to die without completing some of the problems I have in hand. Don't ask me to spend my summer abroad this year—which means postponement of further experiments relating to Aeronautics—not for two or three months—but for a whole year. I cannot do it. I have no objections to you going abroad, no objections to Elsie and Daisy traveling, no objection to Charles the faithful, accompanying you. I would like to go too but I do object to stopping my work here for a year. Better still would be to have you all come here for the summer—rest from the constant excitement of Washington would be good for you all—then in the autumn I will go wherever you want to go.[18]

When Mabel received that letter, she marshaled her strongest arguments:

It would be hard for you to lose a year but think of your child's life spoiled forever for the want of something we can do for her now. I do not mean to say that a foreign journey is a necessity for either of them this year. But I do feel if ever they need our care it is now. After all they have not been very much trouble to

you in the past. I have sent them away to boarding school that you might not have to leave Baddeck. Put the many months that you have had in the past in that way against what you have lost in the last year or two. What I feel is that they cannot find anything in Baddeck to satisfy them this summer. Elsie will think more of Gilbert and Daisy will not have any standard to judge by if her turn comes next winter. Are you willing that Elsie should drift into an engagement with Gilbert without further opportunity of seeing other men? The trip to Japan did a great deal more good in that way than you imagine. I thought that a trip to Europe under your guidance and with the opportunities that you alone can give them might complete the work. At least I would feel that we had done all we could. If after carefully thinking over these arguments you still feel that your own work demands your first consideration, I will say no more. Only remember Elsie and Daisy are also works of yours and that they will live after you. You started them before you started aeronautics so they ought to be finished first![19]

When she realized Alec was adamant about carrying on with his work, she accepted his decision without further protest and took her family to Beinn Bhreagh. As she foresaw, the summer in Baddeck did clinch the matter, and by autumn of 1900 Elsie and Gilbert Grosvenor, familiarly known as Bert, became engaged. In April 1899 he gave up his teaching position in New Jersey to become the associate editor of the magazine put out by the National Geographic Society. They planned to be married in England in October of 1900.

Shortly before the wedding, Mabel wrote to Mrs. Kennan:

I do think I am to be congratulated on my new son. I do not believe it would be possible to find anyone else who would take Elsie so little from me, or who would come so pleasantly and closely into the family himself. We have always been such a united family that it would have been terribly hard to give her to one who, however nice he might be in other respects, would certainly take her away from us in her interests and sympathies. It will be hard enough to let her go when the time comes anyway.

I am not surprised that you should find it hard to believe that she loves Gilbert. She was very slow in making up her mind but early last spring she had come to the knowledge that at least she could not give Gilbert up. Slowly all summer she had grown to the conviction that she could not do without him.[20]

The wedding took place on October 23, 1900, at the Eccleston Square Congregational Church in London, England. This is how Mabel described it to Mrs. Kennan:

The wedding was very nice but oh it cost a lot and I was hoping it would be a quiet inexpensive one. I sent no invitations until after Mr. Bell's arrival a week beforehand, then thought they need only be for the church but was assured that such in England would be considered mean, so added an invitation to breakfast at the hotel. We began with thirty and ended seating seventy at two dollars and something a head, with champagne extra....

Elsie, I thought, never looked more handsome

and never carried herself with such queenly grace, stateliness and perfect composure than on that day as she walked slowly up the broad aisle in her white satin and point lace carrying her head erect under the weight of veil and orange-blossoms. Her bouquet with streamers falling to her feet was of lilies of the valley and white heather, very beautiful and artistic we country people thought.

Elsie is very much in love and thinks there is no one in the world quite so good as Bert. His constant thought for her touches her very deeply and though she refused to promise to obey him at the altar, she is wonderfully submissive to his wishes. Of course, we all had the same feeling that she was fitted for a more brilliant position than Gilbert can give her now, but she is very ambitious to help him to gain one. She thinks it will be all the nicer that she will have to work hand in hand with him to gain it and not simply to accept a fine position obtainable through no exertion of hers. Perhaps she will be all the finer woman for the feeling that her husband is dependent on her help. At all events, she is perfectly happy now.[21]

Mabel's desire that her daughters should have a broad outlook on life prompted this letter to Daisy:

I have been thinking of your going away for Thanksgiving. I think I already told you that you might go but I did not think much about it except that you should be happy. Now, however, I am anxious that you should go for the reason that this is probably your last school year and you may not soon again have another chance to widen your acquaintance with your own people. The people you meet in New York, Boston, Washington and a fashionable place like Morris Plains are not representative Americans. I would think the citizens of Buffalo would be much more so, because Buffalo, while quite a large city, is not a fashionable one, it is more the home of respectable well-to-do cultivated people, the very best class of people. People who live quiet home lives, with enough society to be pleasant but who do not make it their chief business in life as in Washington. I would like you to see how your fellow citizens live out of New York and Washington and hope that you will go.... The increased acquaintances you would gain are as much part of your education as anything else.[22]

When the United States went to war with Cuba in 1898, Miss Clara Barton organized the Red Cross to provide nursing care for wounded American soldiers. Daisy wanted to go on this expedition and Mabel gave her every encouragement. But Alec refused his permission, suggesting an alternative:

My advice is—let her join an Ambulance Class—let her learn how to nurse to begin with and if she chooses, let her have practice in nursing where there is no danger to herself.[23]

Mabel was disappointed. She explained to Elsie:

You will have heard, I suppose, that the Red Cross went [to Cuba] without either Daisy or Mrs. Kennan. I felt relieved that they were not to go but so sorry Daisy was to lose the chance of an entirely new experience under the training of one of the great women of this country.[24]

As a young girl Daisy had been very shy. When she

finished school, she did not wish to come out in society as Elsie had done. When the Cuban expedition fell through it was decided that she should go to New York with her friend Alice Hill and study art with Gutzon Borglum, creator of the giant heads carved in South Dakota's Black Hills. A letter from her mother attempts to come to grips with the age-old problem of propriety:

I have since considered that, as you specifically wrote to Papa that you would "receive no man, not even Robert Marsh [a cousin] in your boarding house," it would please him best to have you write to him again, as he has not replied. Ask him point blank, "Do you really object to my receiving visits from Robert and friends of his whom I have met at Aunt Kitty's and intimate friends of whom she knows all about, and who are quite old and irreproachable, in the public parlor of the boarding house?"

Of course Alice would not have any friends who weren't all right and nice, any more than you, but I think you only want to receive relatives and their friends when they bring them. Thus I think it would be all right for you to receive Mr. Ruhl if he called with Robert but I would rather you didn't if he came alone. The reason in propriety is obvious—you have got Robert to stand by you in such case and Robert is, I think, that kind of a fellow whose conservatism and good sense inspires confidence.

Bother—you know perfectly well where to draw the line yourself. You can put yourself in Papa's and my place perfectly well and act accordingly if you take the trouble to stop and think and be honest. It is only

that having voluntarily made an offer to Papa you should stand by it until he releases you. Write him and I will make him telegraph a reply.[25]

It took more than one letter to guide a vivacious young daughter around the shoals of propriety:

I do not like the idea of your going to Mr. Harris's [an artist whom Alice later married] boarding house. I do not think it is the thing at all. I cannot understand you doing it, or Alice either. I am very sorry. I don't like to think that Alice's judgment is not to be relied upon and that her influence over you is not what I approve of, but it looks that way now.

I cannot see any need of your breaking the conventions so far in order to have a good time. This is a very good world and there are plenty of nice things in it and I believe in thinking the best of everyone, but it is not customary for young ladies to go to a gentleman's boarding house and club and I do not like you doing it.

Alice is not old enough to be your chaperone. She is far better than nobody, that is all, and I feel that she is not helping you steer a safe course now.... I have not said anything to Papa about this or shown him your letters and I would not like to tell anyone that you have been doing these things.

My position is this, I am liberal enough and broadminded enough to go against every convention in the land, if enough is to be gained by doing so, but I cannot see that you are gaining enough to warrant running counter to your mother's and father's feelings of propriety and the feeling of all your family.

If I were with you, half the reason for all this

consideration of convention would not exist, but no one has ever yet invented a way to eat one's cake and have it and you cannot take the freedom of a poor and friendless girl and be also a rich heiress and possessor of a father's and mother's love and care. After all, it would not be justice—there must be some compensation of the poor girl....[26]

I am so distressed to have had to write anything you won't like. My letter must have come like cold water on the red hot steel of your enthusiasm. There must be a sizzling!

Perhaps I can help matters by putting in a few words of my ideas on the matter—I would have you cling with unnecessary strictness to convention in minor matters to balance your disregard of it in important ones. It was unconventional for you to go to the Harris studio that evening but I would have done it myself. What you gained was worthwhile. It was unconventional of you to go to those luncheons—and what you gained was not worthwhile.[27]

In the autumn of 1903 Gilbert Grosvenor made the acquaintance of the distinguished botanist David Grandison Fairchild. Born in 1869 in East Lansing, Michigan, he came from a family of prominent educators. His father, George Fairchild, was professor and acting president of Michigan State Agricultural College for more than twenty years before becoming president of the Kansas State Agricultural College; his grandfather, Grandison Fairchild, had been one of the founders of Oberlin College. After graduating with a master's degree from Kansas State Agricultural College, David studied botany at Rutgers College before going to Europe for further research in Italy and Germany. He directed and participated in many expeditions, collected living plants from all over the world and was personally responsible for introducing more than 75,000 new species, varieties or strains of plants into the United States. The Fairchild Tropical Garden in Coconut Grove, Florida, was named in his honor.

When Grosvenor met him, he had just returned from a trip up the Persian Gulf to Baghdad, and it was arranged that he give a lecture to the National Geographic Society. Grosvenor later took him to one of Dr. Bell's Wednesday evening receptions where distinguished men of science gathered to discuss their chosen subjects. Supper was always served at these receptions and usually attended by Mabel and her daughters. In late November 1904, Daisy, just back from New York, sat next to David Fairchild at one of these gatherings. A romance developed from this chance encounter that culminated in their marriage the following April. For the first year after the wedding they lived in the annex of the Bell home at 1331 Connecticut Avenue until acquiring a forty-acre tract of woodland in Maryland where they built their new home.

Several years later, when accompanying Alec to England where he was being honored by Oxford University, Mabel wrote her mother:

Oh Mama dear, I wish you were with us. Not the least nice thing is to hear about my distinguished son-in-law, David Fairchild, he seems better known abroad than in Washington. Twice people have spoken to Alec of him and his great work, not knowing of his connection with us.[28]

14
The Mature Mabel

ALTHOUGH MABEL WAS ABSORBED in providing her daughters with a proper education, she didn't forget her parents. Hubbard continued to be active in the work of the Association to Promote the Teaching of Speech to the Deaf and served on the board of corporators of the Clarke School, as well as performing his duties as president of the Commission of Scientific Societies of Washington, president of the National Geographic Society and regent of the Smithsonian Institution. Mabel noticed, however, that he preferred spending more and more time quietly at home with his collection of Napoleonic prints and his intimate friends. He was suffering from diabetes, and this hung like a cloud over Mabel and her mother. Mabel stayed with her mother during her father's last illness. She wrote to Mrs. Kennan:

I cannot see why my father should be ill past recovery now. He is not old [seventy-five] as men go nowadays and he has lived such a healthy life.

Thursday at twelve I saw no change and went into town to help Grace arrange the flowers for her tea, anxious but with the Doctor's assurance that all was well. When I came back at five, the change was so great I was horrified. I watched by him for fifteen minutes and it took all my courage not to call my mother to share my watch as it looked as if he were dying then. But he rallied later and next day seemed stronger and we had a little hope.[1]

Hubbard died on December 11, 1897. Mabel wrote Mrs. Kennan:

The end was very quiet and peaceful, a very gentle ceasing to breathe, a quiet falling asleep, and my father never looked more beautiful than just then, the rosy color still lingering in his face.

I cannot believe that he is really gone, it must be all some dreadful nightmare from which I will awake and go and tell Papa and over which he will laugh in his quiet, humorous, amused way. When I think how alive he was, how foreign all this grief and blackness was to him, the two don't go together.

And it is hardly Mama in her plain black gown with the unnatural white at throat and sleeves and all her pretty soft fluffiness gone. She sits there in Papa's chair and tries to carry on her own life and his too and be brave and bright and keep the friends about her he loved, while her eyelids are swollen. Gypsy says she sobs at night when there is no one to see her, when Papa is no longer there to hold her hand and read to her by the hour.

Now she has lost not merely a devoted husband and lover, but also the greatest part of all that made her life interesting. After having been in the midst of life, the companion of many of the cleverest men in the nation, to have to stand aside and have no more part and lot in affairs, to be reduced to the conversation of ordinary women and just one or two men, that will be awfully hard. Still after all there are worse things as Mama herself said. She might have had to watch Papa grow really old, see the clear mind fail, and that she

163

said she could not have endured. That he was to the last himself is her great comfort now.[2]

When Alec went to Beinn Bhreagh the following spring, Mabel remained at Twin Oaks with her mother. Together they went through Hubbard's papers. It came as a revelation to realize all her father had accomplished for the deaf in America. She undertook to prepare an account of his work under the title "The Story of the Rise of the Oral Method in America as told by Mr. Hubbard."

Alec was not well, yet insisted on attending the Annual Conference for the Deaf. Mabel wrote:

Now my darling, I know that you will not let anything cause you to swerve from the path of duty but I cannot believe it can be your duty to commit suicide, nor can I see how the cause of the deaf can be advanced by the death of the only man of very great importance and influence in their ranks. Formerly there was Papa, now you are the only one. There is money back of almost every other field of work. Yours is the only money backing the deaf. You are the leader in the forces of the Oralists and you can lead them from a distance [and not risk your health by attending their Conference].

I thought of going right up to you at Beinn Bhreagh dropping everything and yet as my work progresses, I am filled with an even greater sense of my obligation to my father and mother. I do not want to lose the only chance that will ever be mine to make the only return to them in my power that will seem at all adequate. Yet, if you are ill, I will come, that is first.[3]

While staying with her mother, she wrote to her cousin Lena McCurdy:

Twin Oaks is horribly sad and lonely without my father, yet I love each part of it more than ever before because it is something of him that is left to us. He loved it, he loved the trees and the shrubs and flowers. Most of the arrangement and selection that made the place so beautiful was his. I had always thought it was my mother's doing. I know now that it was at least as much my father's and that from his early childhood the passion for flowers was ingrained. My father would always say "Mrs. Hubbard did so and so," "Mrs. Hubbard's flowers," but I find now from his letters that it was really he who ordered and planned with her help, and for her, but nevertheless of his own volition. And so I love the place and everything on it the more that I am so sorry that they have lost my father's love and care.[4]

When summer came Mabel left Twin Oaks and returned to Alec at Beinn Bhreagh. Arriving there she was struck anew with a sense of grief, as she confided in her mother:

I am home again and it is beautiful and glorious being home but how I miss you and Papa. I have no one to replace Papa, no one who gives me the same sympathetic interest in all my plans for the making of the grounds worthy of the place. Each tree he planted is dearer to me than any other. I have been home but a few hours and I am overwhelmed with the amount of work requiring the master's care. There are things that Alec cares little for but which Papa would have helped me with. I never ceased to miss him daily and hourly at Twin Oaks, I miss him scarcely less at Beinn Bhreagh.[5]

After Hubbard's death Bell became president of the National Geographic Society. During his first year in office he was so preoccupied with his own experimental work at Beinn Bhreagh that he gave little attention to the affairs of the society. Membership dropped from fifteen hundred to a thousand; debts accumulated. Mabel and her mother were anxious that the society, which had meant so much to Hubbard, should prosper. Moreover, they felt strongly that Alec needed the stimulation of the Washington scientific world. Mabel wrote to Mrs. Kennan:

I do not know yet to be glad or sorry that Alec is President of the Geographic Society. Of course it is a complete change and of course he would not have accepted it except for my father's sake. But neither Mama nor I would have been willing he should take it solely on that ground. I have been feeling for some time that he needed to mix more with men for awhile at least and in this way he certainly will. They have nominated Mr. Bell to succeed Papa as Regent of the Smithsonian.[6]

Bell laid aside his experimental work at Beinn Bhreagh, came to Washington to concentrate on the National Geographic Society and threw himself into this enterprise with his usual enthusiasm. Mabel and Daisy shared his interest, suggesting that instead of the dull scientific journal which the society published for its members, a magazine of pictures connected by a few words would be much more interesting.

This suggestion was one of the sources of inspiration that caused Bell to change completely the format of the National Geographic magazine, making it into a bright, interesting non-technical periodical. This resulted in recruiting an enormous membership from the general public. A full-time vigorous, intelligent editor was needed, whose monthly salary of one hundred dollars Bell was prepared to underwrite for a year. The board accepted his offer and Bell persuaded young Gilbert Grosvenor to give up his teaching position in New Jersey and come to Washington as the National Geographic Society's first full-time employee. This he did on April 1, 1899.

Bell's confidence in Gilbert Grosvenor was fully justified by an enormous increase in the magazine's circulation within a comparatively short time; with it the scope and influence of the National Geographic Society grew. As time passed Bell became convinced that the president of the society should be a man with an extensive scientific background, which he felt that he did not possess. He therefore decided to resign. Mabel and Mrs. Hubbard felt that the time was not ripe for such a change. Mabel pleaded with Alec, both for the sake of her father's work and her mother's happiness, that he continue a while longer as president:

Alec Dear, Papa loved this Society. He worked as long and hard on perfecting it as you have on your problems. Wouldn't it seem hard to you if you had to die and leave them and to have Bert refuse to go on and complete them if he could "because he isn't really a scientific man." Don't you think I would feel horribly if I had to stand by and see all your work of years going almost for nothing, not because no one could save it, but because Bert's regard for his own reputation wouldn't allow him to go ahead and finish your work

167

as he could do if he chose? This is just how Mama feels and I feel so badly that it spoils all my pleasure in being with her.

You often say, "Your dear Mama I love her so much I wish I could do something for her," and here is the one thing that you can do for her....

Alec my Darling, I do love you and I don't want to urge anything distasteful on you. I want you to be free to follow your own inclinations but my mother, Alec, my little mother is nearing the end, she can't wait to see things come out right. I do want her last days to be happy and full of love and gratitude to you. I will do my best for your father, do your best for my mother.[7]

Bell continued his association with the National Geographic Society for the rest of his life. Full management, first of the magazine, then of the society, was transferred gradually to Gilbert Grosvenor. For over fifty years he directed the affairs of the National Geographic Society successfully, succeeded as editor by his son and grandson. Mabel's interest in the society continued throughout her life.

After Elsie and Daisy were married to fine young men whom Alec and Mabel respected and enjoyed, Mabel was no longer torn between the demands of her husband and those of her daughters. Much of the tension that had grown up between husband and wife over the past years disappeared, and she was happy to concentrate most of her energies in assisting and encouraging Alec with his work. For the first time in her life she was truly interested in Alec's work for the deaf and offered her help:

Alec Dear, I never was so in love with the work [for the deaf] as now that I have been going over the history of the founding of the Clarke School. But the more I see what remains to be done, the less I want you to exhaust yourself now. Why can't I represent you? I will open the house [in Washington] and with Elsie's and Daisy's help will entertain people and read your Report. I will talk as I never did with Miss Yale and Miss Fuller [distinguished teachers of the deaf]. Surely I can do something—try me—try your daughters. If anything happened to you, we would be all that was left to carry on the work. Stand aside this time and see what we can do.[8]

Along with his work for the deaf, for years Bell had been obsessed with his flying machine experiments. Mabel explained to her mother:

I have tried to tie Alec down to tell me his plans. He is very unsatisfactory. He said he would not leave his flying machine experiments until they are in a more satisfactory shape than now. He can't carry them on anywhere else but at Beinn Bhreagh and he can do nothing else until they are finished. They are killing him but he won't leave them and he won't stop. It is cruel of me to try and make him leave.

I had hoped he could find work to do in his Washington laboratory that would keep him contented there. He has work that he could better carry on there than here but he says he must wait for the completion of his flying machine experiments. Alec thinks these are the hardest, slowest, most tiresome and most unsatisfactory experiments that he has ever attempted and the most discouraging but he will not give up until he has got some results.[9]

Mabel had already suggested that he should have help with his work, but in a letter Alec explained to her why he was not yet ready for such assistance:

I cannot carry this work on much further alone—as my eyes have given out—I feel that the strain is too great for me to work at these curves as laboriously as I have done in the past—without the assistance of younger eyes and brains.

You must remember that this is not a question of invention but DISCOVERY—and discovery is groping if you will—a slow laborious systematic groping after knowledge—disheartening in the number of blind alleys explored—and yet this process of groping carefully and systematically all round, in every direction, must lead at last to full knowledge and the discovery of the true path.

No man who has not tackled a difficult subject by himself can understand how much discouraging and disheartening work is necessary in order to achieve success. I begin to appreciate and understand the wonderful labor of Professor Langley in producing his memoir *Experiments in Aerodynamics*. I want too to bring my experiments to a conclusion and can do so here if I am left alone. Then will come the work of invention and then will be the time when I can follow your suggestion of having half a dozen men or more in my laboratory instead of two. But now I could not tell them what to do.[10]

The great problem confronting Bell at this time was how a heavy engine, let alone a man, could be supported by a machine in the air. Surprising as it may seem, his inspiration came from a trivial thing—children's flying kites. He experimented with kites of all types: box, cartwheels, circles, triangles and finally tetrahedral—a kite cell with four triangular faces. Local women were employed at Beinn Bhreagh to stitch scarlet silk on thousands of frames, which made the kites look like a great flock of red birds. It must have been a strange sight to see the elderly Bell with his flowing white beard racing up and down the hills with his workmen hauling as many as fifty kites of various shapes and sizes bobbing behind them in the wind. Mabel wrote to Alec:

I am growing so impatient to hear of your giant kite. I wish I could be with you when you first try it. My Dear, I do appreciate all the wonderful unfailing uncomplaining patience that you have shown in all your work and the quiet persistent courage with which you have gone on after one failure after another. How many there have been, how often an experiment from which you hoped great things has proved contrary. How very, very few and far apart have been your successes. Yet nothing has been able to shake your faith, to stop you in your work. I think it is wonderful and I do admire and love you more as the years go by. But oh, how I wish that you may have success at last. Cannot you import other carpenters from Sydney? I wish you would get some so that your great kite may the sooner be done. Don't delay for the sake of money. Never mind if we have to sell stocks, I can't have you wear your life out waiting for the slow movement of one or two workmen.[11]

On occasion Mabel made some practical suggestions that were of great help in his experiments. This item was in Bell's *Home Notes*, his daily record:

Two great successes scored today, both as a result of suggestions of Mabel's. 1. Instead of waiting for wind—attach kites to galloping horses. Tried it yesterday with a small kite. Result so promising that we tried three of our large kites today in the same way—or nearly so—and could judge of their way of falling better than with wind. 2. How to fasten wires together to make skeleton of a regular tetrahedron and how to fasten these tetrahedra together. Mabel suggested sealing wax. Have tried it and have found it the thing for models. Sealing wax may be useful even on kites. While brittle in thin sheet—or when thin—it is remarkably solid in a globular form. It is like glass—sheets of glass very brittle, but boys' glass marbles stand all sorts of rough usage.[12]

Mabel wrote to her son-in-law Bert:

The storm Father wanted [to fly his giant kite] came last Friday, a week ago today, and because the bay was impossible, only Ferguson who drove around with MacIver appeared. They never tried to get the others over or send word to Father that the other workmen hadn't come. They let him come down full of excitement and all wrought up to try his great experiment for which he had been waiting a year and for which the new kite house had been especially built. The shock was terrible for Father. He looked gray when he came home, wrote a short note dismissing the staff and closing the laboratory, turned his face to the wall and never spoke again that day or night. The

storm continued the next day. Father got out of bed and with the aid of the men on the place, he himself got the model kite up and the experiment was so satisfactory that it demonstrates that this form of kite could sustain a much greater weight than he had dared hope.

Father had made all his arrangements to leave just one month from now and he would not ask to remain longer than until the next twenty-five-mile-an-hour blow. Then he would go down at least content to have tried his experiment. It wouldn't be so hard if Father was a younger, more active man but he counts every day now. He generally feels well and bright and full of ideas and he is so happy with them but he had such a hard time last year. I am just beginning to take my courage in my hands again and to feel that Father is growing himself again and now I dread the consequences of his leaving [for Washington]. I don't want to go with him because that would make his return still more difficult, yet I am ready to make a great fight to give him his chance. I won't have him made to leave just as he is stretching to grasp his prize for which he has struggled and worked so many years so patiently and uncomplainingly. It is strange how many times he has had to leave just in this way and he admits getting superstitious about it.[13]

15
The Aerial Experiment Association

MANY OF BELL'S INVENTIONS, conceived over a period of almost thirty years, required a great deal of improvement to be of any commercial value. They ranged from toys to utility instruments for use in various trades and professions. For example, the phonograph made for Elsie when she was a baby, when spun like a top, emitted distinct musical notes and spoke words. Bell considered that he had brought this to within measurable distance of being patentable, but shrank from the idea of appearing in the patent office as the inventor of a plaything. Then there was a surveying device for finding levels by means of a water hose, and the induction probe for detecting bullets or pieces of metal in the human body painlessly. This device could also be used for discovering metals hidden in the ground or under water.

As Bell so often explained to Mabel, he had worked his ideas far enough to be assured in his own mind of their practicability and did not want to waste valuable time fussing with them further when there were so many other things demanding his attention. Mabel worried that this same attitude would result with the kites and flying machines that had so engaged his thoughts during the past twenty years.

Apart from the kites, from which Bell hoped to develop a man-carrying flying machine, the invention that captured Mabel's imagination was his tetrahedral construction system for which he had already obtained letters patent. The system, based on fitting together four-foot tetrahedral cells made of half-inch iron pipe, formed a structure of remarkable lightness, strength and rigidity. It could be easily assembled from mass-produced parts without skilled labour.

She believed the system had great possibilities for adaptation in a variety of ways and discussed its potential with various engineers she knew in Washington and Boston. They made her realize it would need thorough testing before offering it for commercial use. Talking the matter over with Alec, they decided that if they built a tower on top of their mountain that could withstand the sweep of wind across the Bras d'Or Lakes, surely that would provide an adequate enough test to encourage commercial enterprises to use it for engineering structures.

In the early spring of 1906, Mabel wrote to Mr. McCurdy's son Douglas, who was studying engineering at the University of Toronto, suggesting that he invite some young friend to Baddeck who would be interested in what Dr. Bell was doing. Douglas forgot Mrs. Bell's suggestion until he was packing to leave for home when his friend Frederick W. Baldwin, known as Casey, drifted into his room to say good-bye. He invited him home for a couple of weeks. Casey had only a vague idea where Baddeck was, but it sounded like a lark, so he agreed to come. Three days later they arrived and were soon caught up in the fascination of Dr. Bell and his kites. Likewise, Bell was impressed by the brilliant young man from Ontario.

175

Although Baldwin had planned on staying for a couple of weeks, he was to remain for forty years.

Bell told Casey about his idea of building a tower on top of the mountain based on his tetrahedral construction system and invited him to work on the project. Mabel wrote to Daisy:

Father and Mr. Baldwin are wild over steel tetrahedrons. For the first time in his life Father is associated with a purposeful man of ability, one whose attitude toward him is not that of a paid employee but of a graduate of a technical school. He is to study under him with the idea of working out Papa's ideas along practical lines. Mr. Baldwin begins tomorrow on the construction of a steel tetrahedral tower eighty feet high on the top of the mountain. He expects to get the whole thing up with just a jackscrew instead of the expensive and complicated machinery usually necessary, so perfectly are the cells fitted one into another.

Father and he have just gone over to the laboratory on foot at 10:00 P.M. to look over the tower model to make sure of some last detail. If only I had a third daughter, she should have this young fellow—but he seems to have no thought but tetrahedrons.[1]

The following summer, after receiving his engineering degree, Douglas McCurdy returned to Baddeck and joined Bell and his friend Baldwin. Their activities must have appeared strange and amusing to the locals who watched them tow kite models with motorboats when the breeze was right, measure wind velocities and altitudes, test engines and propellers plus a host of other experiments.

They were joined by twenty-five-year-old Lieutenant Thomas E. Selfridge, a graduate of West Point. He had heard of Bell's experiments with flying machines and came to Beinn Bhreagh to see them for himself. He had the vision to see that some day flying machines would become an important branch of the military. After their first interview in Washington, Bell arranged with President Roosevelt to have Selfridge detailed to come to Baddeck as an observer for the U.S. Army.

Needing a light engine for the big kite, Bell approached Glenn H. Curtiss of Hammondsport, New York, a young motorcycle manufacturer who held the world's record for the fastest mile ever made in any machine, won with a motorcycle of his own design and manufacture. Curtiss's father had died when his son was six; Glenn had no brothers and his only sister was deaf. He had become a dour man whose few joys in life were machinery and speed. He came to Beinn Bhreagh in September to fit the engine Bell had ordered for his kite and became interested in what was being attempted. Although he did not share the comradeship enjoyed by the other three young men, he did have a rapport with Mabel, possibly because of his deaf sister.

Over the years, by constantly sharing the thoughts of her husband, Mabel Bell acquired an amazing grasp of scientific subjects such as few women of her day could have possessed. Because she understood her husband so thoroughly, she was able not only to contribute to his success, but also to play an important role herself in the development of the airplane. She understood her husband's genius and his limitations.

Watching these four young men, each with his own different ability, working so happily with Alec, she realized that this was the kind of association she had wanted for him for years. She had recently received $20,000 from the sale of a piece of property in Washington that she had inherited from her father. Unlike most of her financial resources that came from the telephone shares, she felt this money to be her very own, to do with as she wished. Why shouldn't she use it to finance an association that would include Alec and the four young men? They could work together developing a flying machine based on Alec's tetrahedral construction system. After giving the matter a great deal of thought, she broached the subject. All five men were enthusiastic. Bell felt that they should not limit themselves to the tetrahedral construction alone, but endeavor, by any means possible, to get a man into the air. Mabel agreed. The Aerial Experiment Association came into existence on October 1, 1907, for a term of one year.

Mabel provided the capital up to $20,000. Bell offered the use of his laboratory and other facilities without charge. It was agreed that Bell would serve as chairman without salary; Baldwin and McCurdy would get $1,000 a year, and Curtiss $5,000 a year when on the scene and half that amount when away. It was realized that his own business commitments would not permit him to give the A.E.A. his full time. Selfridge, already on full pay as an army officer, declined a salary.

Bell pointed out to his associates that, based on his experience with the telephone, they could not hope for great financial returns from the construction of flying machines as litigation over patent rights would destroy profit for many years. The chief inducement to keep them together would be the actual accomplishment of aerial flight and the honor and glory that would belong to those who succeeded.

They agreed that the energies of the A.E.A. should be directed first to the completion of the tetrahedral man-carrying kite, the *Cygnet*, already near completion at Beinn Bhreagh. Afterwards, each associate in turn should have the assistance of the others in the construction of a machine according to his own design.

Although Curtiss had to return to his business in Hammondsport, Baldwin, McCurdy and Selfridge lived with the Bells at Beinn Bhreagh, sharing the family life while working on the completion of the man-carrying kite. Mabel sent her mother a description of their life together:

We are having a really good time all by our-selves. The three young fellows here are as nice as they can possibly be and a hundred times less trouble than girls to entertain. They are out of the house all day and seem perfectly content to remain indoors in the evening. The only time they have been away has been to attend a Yacht Club meeting. They are so nice to me. I like the Lieutenant very much indeed, he is very appreciative of everything one does for him. My boys are all such good friends and yet so different, such jolly boys off duty, all so full of fun and all so earnest when it's time for work....

We are very much encouraged over the latest experiments. Alec is now ready to abandon floats and aim directly at turning the kite into a man-carrying flying machine. He knows how to send a kite into the air from the water and how to receive it from the air. These are the two things he wanted solved before he would allow

179

anyone to try riding a kite-flying machine.[2]

On December 12, 1907, Mabel stood on the upper deck of the local steamer *Blue Hill*, which the A.E.A. had hired to tow their catamaran barge. On it rested the *Cygnet*, looking like a huge wedge of honeycomb with its hundreds of tetrahedral-shaped cells that the local women had taken months to cover with red silk.

The honor of making the flight had been given to Selfridge; Baldwin and McCurdy helped him crawl in the culvert-like hole that served as the cockpit. There he lay, face downward, able to see only what was directly in front of him. When all was ready Baldwin and McCurdy joined their workmen on the *Blue Hill*. One man was delegated to cut the tow line with an axe if any emergency should arise. Bell followed with the motor launch in case of an accident.

He gave the signal to start. The steamer headed into the wind and slowly the great kite took to the air, soaring immediately to a height of 168 feet where it flew with great steadiness for several minutes in the stiff breeze. It retained a level keel through all the gusts, at times seeming glued to one spot in the sky. Finally, during a sudden lull in the wind, it descended, alighting on the water so gently and evenly that its passenger was not aware of what was happening.

Unfortunately, in the excitement of the moment and because of blinding smoke that just then belched from the towing steamer, no one cut the tow line and the floating kite was dragged violently through the water and destroyed. When Selfridge felt the fragile craft breaking up he managed to crawl out of the cockpit and plunge into the icy water. Although dressed in oil skins, he was not wear-

180

ing his boots and was able to swim clear. Bell became so concerned for Selfridge's safety that for a moment he did not realize that his dream of getting the *Cygnet* into the air with an engine had been completely shattered.

The people of Baddeck, many of whom watched from the shore, were so thrilled that the first flight of a man and kite had taken place in their village that they presented Dr. Bell with a piece of silver to commemorate the event.

This experiment ended work at Beinn Bhreagh for that year. As the season was now too far advanced for further outdoor work and the laboratory staff was fully occupied manufacturing new tetrahedral cells to replace those destroyed in the *Cygnet* disaster, it was decided to accept Curtiss's invitation to visit Hammondsport and use his workshop and tools.

In January 1908, the Bells returned to Washington while the three young men joined Curtiss at Hammondsport. Although Bell only got to Hammondsport at irregular intervals, he kept in close touch with all that was going on by establishing a weekly bulletin; this continued until the association terminated in March 1909. The *A.E.A. Bulletin* contained over two thousand pages of valuable data on aeronautical experiments, not all of it confined to the work of the association itself.

That winter in Hammondsport the young associates carried out their first gliding experiments based on the Chanute type of glider. The knowledge they obtained was applied in building their first motor-driven machine. The gliders were so crude that soft snow provided a welcome protection. A light biplane structure was designed that fitted over the shoulders yet allowed the experimenter's feet to remain free for running. The would-be birdman raced down a steep slope hoping for sufficient speed to lift him off the ground. Occasionally they made it into the air, but the glider lacked stability. Adding a tail structure improved matters considerably. After this, flights of thirty or forty yards were not uncommon, and on one occasion McCurdy recorded a flight of over one hundred yards.[3]

The first machine to be built was Selfridge's *Red Wing*, so called because of its silk wing covering, the same red as the kites. On March 12, 1908, when conditions were right for a test, Selfridge happened to be absent on business and Baldwin was chosen to go.

On the frozen surface of Lake Keuka, near Hammondsport, the *Red Wing* had been fitted with iron sleigh runners to facilitate its takeoff. Curtiss, McCurdy and several of the factory workmen were on skates, which was fortunate because when the engine started the plane moved off with no one inside to control it. The men on skates went racing after it and brought it back to the starting point. Baldwin climbed into the cockpit. Several men grasped the wings, holding the plane back as the engine revved up. Then Casey yelled, "Let her go!" and the *Red Wing* was off, roaring across the ice.

She rose easily on the light breeze and sailed through the air 319 feet until Baldwin brought her down to a smooth landing. This was the first flight by a Canadian and the first public flight of a flying machine in North America. Earlier flights by the Wright Brothers had been made privately.

Five days later Baldwin again took the *Red Wing* up, but this time she caught in a breeze and came down heavily, demolishing the wings. The crash proved to Casey that shifting the pilot's weight was not enough to keep the machine stable. In designing the A.E.A.'s second plane, Baldwin's *White Wing*, he incorporated hinged tips, or ailerons, into the wings, connected by wires to the pilot's seat. Now when the plane tilted it could be corrected by the pilot.

After Baldwin's successful flight in the *Red Wing*, the Aero Club of America held a banquet in his honor, at which Bell refused to take any credit for the success of the experiment and paid tribute to the four young men of the Aerial Experiment Association. The *White Wing* was flown successfully by Baldwin, Selfridge and Curtiss, before McCurdy crashed her beyond repair.

The third A.E.A. machine, Curtiss's *June Bug*, at first seemed to have little lift. Suspecting that air was leaking through the porous cotton, the associates smeared the fabric with linseed oil, thereby doping the wings of a flying machine for the first time.

Upon their return to Beinn Bhreagh in June 1908, Alec and Mabel stopped over at Hammondsport. She described their activities: "The sun is warm, but the air is exhilarating and everywhere they are working and working at new things. They are young and their work is the youth of a great new thing in the history of the world."[4]

The associates had originally planned to resume work on the tetrahedral aerodrome *Cygnet II* at Beinn Bhreagh early in the spring. But Bell was detained in Washington, and since the project required his personal supervision it was decided to utilize the time by constructing a fourth plane at Hammondsport called the *Silver*

Dart. The trials with the three earlier machines had demonstrated the need for a more powerful engine than the eight-cylinder air-cooled Curtiss motor they had been using. It would take time before Curtiss could provide a special water-cooled motor. Accordingly, the associates divided their forces, Baldwin accompanying Bell to Beinn Bhreagh while McCurdy and Selfridge remained at Hammondsport to work on the *Silver Dart*.

The Scientific American Trophy had been offered for the first successful flight of heavier-than-air machine flying a measured kilometer under set conditions. On July 4, 1908, at Hammondsport, the A.E.A. undertook to try for this coveted award with the *June Bug* piloted by Curtiss. Among the many interested spectators who came up from New York and Washington for the event were Daisy and David Fairchild. Daisy wrote to her parents at Beinn Bhreagh:

In spite of all I have read and heard, and all the photographs I have seen, the actual sight of a man flying past me through the air was thrilling to a degree that I can't express. We all lost our heads. David shouted and I cried, and everybody cheered and clapped and engines hooted....

The banks were crowded with spectators, but the flight on the 4th for the Trophy was not as well attended as the one on the 5th as the weather was so uncertain. It showered and blew all day until about six o'clock when it cleared and ideal flying conditions prevailed. Before that, much of the time was taken up with measuring the course. No very pleasant task through a wet meadow, plowed potato patch and

swamps. David started off immaculate in his white clothes and came back a sorry sight.

At the first flight, I was at the corner of the vineyard nearest the road with Douglas, and David was at the starting line. The machine rose beautifully and flew by us, but didn't quite make the kilometer. It was flying pretty high and Mr. Curtiss wanted to bring it down but she didn't answer her controls quickly, and when he got her down, he couldn't get her up again. Nothing was hurt, and all hands towed her back to the starting point. For the second flight, David, Mrs. Curtiss and I chose our stand on the old log at the far side of the potato patch.

The first flight raised excitement to the boiling point, and as Mr. Curtiss flew over the red flag that marked the finish and away on toward the trees, I don't think any of us quite knew what we were doing. One lady was so absorbed as not to hear the coming train and was struck by the engine and had two ribs broken.[5]

David Fairchild, writing of this event in his book *The World Was My Garden*, had this to say:

That brief afternoon at Hammondsport had changed my vision of the world as it was to be. There was no longer the shadow of doubt in my mind that the sky would be full of aeroplanes and that the time would come when people would travel through the air faster and more safely than they did on the surface of the earth.[6]

In August Lieutenant Selfridge was ordered back to Washington and posted to the Signal Corps. As a result of the expert knowledge gained through his association with the A.E.A., he was made a member of the newly formed Aeronautical Board of the U.S. Army. A few weeks later, to his great delight, he was chosen to accompany Orville Wright on one of the test flights being conducted at Fort Myer, Virginia, for the government. The world may no longer remember that disastrous flight of September 17, 1908. Wright was seriously hurt and Selfridge died as a result of his injuries. He became the first casualty in American aviation history.

When news of the disaster reached Beinn Bhreagh, Bell and Baldwin set off immediately for Washington. The following day Mabel wrote to Alec:

I can't get over Tom being taken. I simply can't realize it—it doesn't seem possible. Isn't it heartbreaking? Yet, it is better for him than to die as poor Langley did [of a broken heart because of the ridicule of the press when he failed in his attempt to fly his machine]. He was so happy to the very end. I know he would have said he was having the time of his life although he must have realized his danger; those last seconds he would still hope to escape and he had no time for unavailing regrets. I miss the thought of him so much. Nobody ever did so many little things for me as he. Others have loved me more, of course, but he just saw the little things, pushing up my chair to the table or bringing a screen to shut off drafts, all so quietly and unobtrusively that no one noticed. I am so sorry for you dear, in this breaking of our beautiful Association. But it was beautiful and the memory of it will endure.

Bell, Curtiss, Baldwin, McCurdy and Selfridge,

it was indeed a "brilliant coterie" as one paper has said. Do anything you think best but let the A.E.A. be only those to the end, and then take some other name. Give my love to them all and let's hold tight together, all the tighter for the one that is gone. Casey calls me the "little mother of us all" and so I want to be. I love all our boys and there can't be any others just the same.[7]

The association's original term would end in a few days. The *Silver Dart* was still at Hammondsport and practically complete. Bell wanted to try it out on the ice at Beinn Bhreagh. He decided to carry on the association for another six months from October 1, 1908, until March 31, 1909.

On February 23, 1909, McCurdy flew the *Silver Dart* a distance of half a mile over the ice in the presence of all the townspeople of Baddeck. It was the first flight by a British subject of a heavier-than-air machine in the British Empire. Mabel described it all to Daisy:

Another perfect day, the *Silver Dart* made a short flight, coming down because the land was near, she had to go across the bay on account of a baby wind. We all pleaded hard with Papa for another flight but he was firm. It was the first flight of an airship in Canada and he would take no chance of disaster to spoil this first success. All Baddeck was out in sleighs or on skates. We had to wait two hours and they whiled away the time with horse races up and down the smooth hard ice. Can you realize people dashing up and down feeling perfectly secure with only a foot or so of ice between them and forty feet of water? I just love Baddeck these glorious winter days—you poor Southerners know nothing of their exhilaration.[8]

That first flight was followed by others made nearly daily while the ice held. Mabel described them:

It was a really wonderful flight Douglas made this morning. He started about 100 yards from the boathouse, out on the bay and flew across toward Kennan's boathouse and thence toward the lighthouse making a glorious sweep, and came back past Beinn Bhreagh shore passing close to me purposely as I said I hadn't really seen yesterday's flight—swept out of sight on the tongue of land which forms the entrance to the harbor—way up the bay. Unfortunately he miscalculated the space there for making the return curve and he was obliged to make a bad landing to avoid trees. In the air six minutes—beautiful sight.[9]

A few weeks later in Washington Mabel wrote Alec:

I wish you would send me copies of your dictation so I can know what your experiments are and what you are thinking of. What do you think of the results of Douglas's flights? Is the motor going to be reliable? If not, won't you get another, even an automobile motor if that will carry the *Silver Dart*. I consider that the success of the *Silver Dart* means everything to us in the prestige it gives to all our work. I have spent all the money and more than I got from my property, still I do want you to go on and put more of your money into the venture so as to assure the success of the *Silver Dart* and its purchase by governments. I'd a hundred times rather have Mr. Curtiss's motor succeed than any other, but still the first thing is the success of the aerodome. Nothing succeeds like success you know.

Oh my darling, I wish I were with you all. I

grudge being away these last days of the A.E.A.[10]

While all these experiments were taking place, Alec and Mabel were giving a great deal of thought as to how the work of the association could continue after the March 31 deadline. Mabel had already increased her financial contribution from the original $20,000 to $35,000. Some other financing had to be found. In the *A.E.A. Bulletin*, Bell outlined his ideas of incorporating a joint stock company to manufacture aerodromes and suggested that, since Curtiss had the most extensive business experience, he should be its manager.

It came as a great shock to Mabel and the other association members to learn of the Herring-Curtiss Company formed for the manufacture of heavier-than-air machines. Baldwin, writing in the *A.E.A. Bulletin*, commented:

That level-headed American businessmen should back Mr. Herring has created quite a furor in aeronautical circles. It probably means that Mr. Herring has some more convincing arguments than he ever made public or—it is really the Curtiss Company with Mr. Herring's patents to flourish in the eyes of the bewildered capitalists.[11]

March 6, Bell sent Curtiss the following telegram:

Please write fully concerning your arrangements with Herring and how it affects the relations with A.E.A.[12]

The letter Bell received in reply stated:

I found Mr. Herring quite anxious to close the deal with me and I finally made him an offer, a little better than his original proposition.

Mr. Herring showed me a great deal, and I

189

would not be at all surprised if his patents, backed by a strong company, would pretty well control the use of gyroscope in sustaining automatic equilibrium. This seems to be about the only road to success in securing automatic stability in an aeroplane.

If the deal goes through, I will be the manager of the company and everything will go on just as it has, except that we will have Mr. Herring's devices on the machines which we may build. By the way, that reminds me, I have accepted an order from the Aeronautical Society for an aeroplane to be delivered in the spring at Morris Park, N.Y. I did this on my own responsibility with the idea that if the consolidation was made with Herring, it would be turned over to the new Company, or if a commercial organization succeeded the A.E.A., the order could be turned over to them. If neither of these materialized, the Curtiss Company would endeavor to fill the order itself.[13]

When a concerned Mabel read this letter it prompted Bell to send Curtiss this telegram:

Have your business arranged so as to be here March 31st sure. Very important and you will regret it all your life if not.[14]

On the night of March 31, 1909, a pathetic little group gathered around the great fireplace in the hall at Beinn Bhreagh. Only three of the original members were present: Bell, Baldwin and McCurdy. Mrs. Baldwin, Bell's secretary Mr. Cox, and his assistant, Miss Mabel McCurdy, were invited to join the little group.

McCurdy, the association's secretary, read the following resolution:

Whereas, the members of the Aeronautical Experimental Association individually and collectively feel that Mrs. Alexander Graham Bell has, by her great personal support and inspiring ideas, contributed very materially to any success that the Association may have attained.

Resolved that we place on record our highest appreciation of her loving and sympathetic devotion without which the work of the Association would have come to naught.

It is reluctantly moved by Mr. Baldwin and regretfully seconded by the Secretary that we dissolve.[15]

By the stroke of twelve midnight, the A.E.A. as an association was no more.

16
The Intervening Years

EVER SINCE HER FATHER'S DEATH Mabel had tried to spend as much time as possible with her mother, but she hated to be away from Alec. She wrote him:

It just gets harder and harder to leave you every time. I do love you so. We depend on each other more and more as time goes on. You make almost the whole of my life now.[1]

However, she always enjoyed Washington in the

early spring. In 1909, driving with her mother in her new car was an added source of pleasure:

Been for a first drive with Mama in her new "Peerless" [car], it is indeed luxury embodied. It cost $5,000 and I can't see but it is well worth the money as anything except a house or an estate. I should rather have it than a motor launch. With all due respect to Casey, somehow I feel safer on land than on sea. I wonder whether the time will come in our lifetime when we will feel as safe and fare as luxuriously moving through the air? I have no doubt that the time will come for people now living but how nice if you and I could see it and enjoy it. You and I sitting together while our chauffeur steers us through the air up and down with great smooth motionless sweeps.[2]

Bell was invited to address the Canadian Club in Ottawa on March 27, 1909, and speak about the experiments carried out by the Aerial Experiment Association. He welcomed this invitation, considering it of great importance to the future of the associates that the A.E.A.'s achievements should be heard at a national gathering that included such eminent people as Earl Grey, the governor general, Prime Minister Sir Wilfrid Laurier, a number of cabinet ministers and other distinguished guests. Replying to Alec's account of the event, Mabel wrote:

Of course you found the Ottawa trip fatiguing but what an experience! How delightful to move a large audience of worthwhile men to enthusiasm! This is one of the things you can do as few men can and you must enjoy the doing of it.[3]

A short time later Baldwin and McCurdy, with fi-

192

nancial backing from the Bells, formed the Canadian Aerodrome Company for the purpose of manufacturing flying machines, with headquarters at Beinn Bhreagh. In their first year they built *Baddeck No. 1* and *No. 2*. With these two aerodromes, and the *Silver Dart*, they hoped to demonstrate the importance of flying machines to the Canadian government and obtain contracts for their construction.

The Canadian government invited them to give a demonstration on the art of flying at the army's camp at Petawawa near Ottawa. They shipped the *Silver Dart* and *Baddeck No. 1* to Petawawa by train. On the morning of August 2, 1909, before an audience of army officers and government officials, the *Silver Dart* made five separate flights, flying fifty miles an hour at an altitude of about fifty feet. All flights were successful until the fifth. McCurdy, unfamiliar with the sandy soil conditions on the cavalry field over which they were flying, and blinded by the sun, misjudged his clearance. The front wheel struck the edge of a sand knoll, and the *Silver Dart* was damaged beyond repair. Fortunately, McCurdy was not seriously injured.

Immediately after the crash Baldwin and McCurdy assembled the *Baddeck No. 1* and within a week it was ready for trials. On August 12 it made a successful short flight, but McCurdy had trouble with the ignition switch and was forced to curtail demonstrations. Next day another flight was attempted, but the machine proved tail heavy and after a flight of about seventy yards slid to earth backwards, doing considerable damage to the plane.

Mabel and Alec were at Beinn Bhreagh at the time, and Mabel wrote her mother:

We are living so quietly I hardly know ourselves.

Alec's and my great excitement is our boys at Petawawa. Alec feels dreadfully over the last accident. It doesn't mean that the *Baddeck No. 1* isn't all that we have believed it, only that it hasn't been tried out before and the various parts want adjustment and perhaps slight alteration. They would not have meant anything here but of course at Petawawa before the eyes of the General Staff, those accidents were very unfortunate and will make it more difficult for the boys to get their contracts.[4]

The following day she wrote Daisy:

The *Toronto Star* telegraphed to know what Father had to say about the *Baddeck No. 1* failure. He replied it was one of the finest aerodromes ever built but that a novel device never before employed was used on it and possibly it was not properly adjusted.

Father and I have concluded that the curved front control was the cause of the accident. It, having greater lifting power than the plane surface to which Douglas is accustomed, would cause the machine to rise with dangerous rapidity in front and not having as great descending power would not act as effectively as the old one. So it would be impossible for Douglas to check the backward tilt.[5]

In spite of these setbacks the two young partners continued their experiments. Governor General Earl Grey had been following their achievements with great interest, and in October 1909, he made a trip to Baddeck to witness for himself the flights of a flying machine. He was invited to stay at Beinn Bhreagh. Unfortunately, the day before his arrival, Mrs. Hubbard was killed in a motor car accident. Alec and Mabel departed immediately for Washington, leaving Casey and Mrs. Baldwin to receive their distinguished guests.

Alec returned to Beinn Bhreagh after the funeral, leaving Mabel at Twin Oaks to help her sister dismantle the Hubbard home. Mabel's feeling were revealed in her letters:

Nobody was as proud of me as she was, nobody else ever made the most of any bright little thing I ever did or said. It is growing more and more strange to have to do without that underlying sense of her love of and pride in me which has lain deep down at the bottom of my heart and comforted me in my moments of deepest depression. "Mama would see, mama would care," and it didn't matter that she really neither knew nor cared, I had but to tell her to get all the sympathy and understanding I wanted.[6]

Charlie and Grace [Bell] are going to take Mama's house. I am almost sorry, it seems to me as if we might perhaps have taken it for our winter home, but after all, it means much more to them.

Most of the important things have been divided up. We got through it with mutual good will instead of quarrels. At one time I thought Gracie [Berta's daughter] and I were in for a fight, but I guess it will work out all right. You know I have taken the Corot [Jean Corot painting], paying $12,000 to the estate for it. I hope you won't object. I would never buy anything very handsome myself because you don't care for such things. I can't buy them alone so this is my only chance.

We gave Bert a silver sword that always lay on

Mama's library table. It was very valuable. It had a beautifully chased silver sheath and we all thought Bert would be just overwhelmed but all he said was, "a sword seems such a queer memento of such a gentle lady."[7]

Mrs. Hubbard left a bequest to the Clarke School for the Deaf to build a memorial hall in memory of her husband. The most important part of the memorial hall was the chapel, and Mabel contributed an additional sum so that all the appointments would be of the best. In it she arranged for a tablet to be placed in memory of her mother, with the inscription, "Whose resolute love gave the blessing of speech to her own little deaf child and formed the inspiration of her husband's effort to secure the same blessing for all other deaf children." The memorial hall was dedicated early in 1913. When still in the planning stage, Mabel wrote to Miss Yale, the principal:

While I like the idea of linking Mama's name more particularly with the Chapel, my original and my chief purpose [in making this contribution] was to make the room bearing her name a sort of capstone to the whole Memorial. The whole building is a memorial to her and my father. The largest and finest room in it is the Chapel and it should be the most beautiful part of it all as she was the most beautiful part of the partnership which was their life.[8]

After the Hubbard home had been dismantled, Mabel thankfully returned to Beinn Bhreagh and buried her grief amidst all the activities.

As long as the ice held, Casey and Douglas continued to fly their remaining machine, the *Baddeck No. 2*.

Major Maunsall, a member of the militia council, was sent to Baddeck in 1910 by the War Department of the Canadian government to report on the progress being made. At the same time the lieutenant governor of Nova Scotia, the Honorable D.C. Fraser, and his son traveled to Baddeck and witnessed these early flights. Mabel wrote to Daisy:

Yesterday was a day as is a day—a beauty, a dandy of a day—and—that old motor chose to balk! It would go for six minutes and then gradually lose power so that the aerodrome would come down. It came down just as if Douglas had meant it to come down—perfectly—on an even keel without jar or flutter—but inexorably down. It was the same old motor that had previously given easy records of fifteen to thirty minutes and had offered more—and no one could discover why it wouldn't go yesterday. It was cold to be sure, but it has been in as cold weather and has not minded. However, the flights that were made were dandies. His Honor the Lieutenant Governor, who didn't know better, was wild with delight and he said he would stand up for them [Baldwin and McCurdy] in Ottawa, and Major Maunsall will also, I am sure.

We had a very pleasant or rather I might say, very interesting week, for both the Major and the Lieutenant Governor are unusual people. The Lieutenant Governor looked as if he had just stepped out of a historical picture. There he was—stout old Peter Stuyvesant come to life—so big and burly with his great tall cane and cape and immense fur gauntlets— stalking around, master of all, and everyone very much at his service. And Douglas, the very ideal of the

trim-knit wiry young coureur de bois, standing before the bluff old Governor straight and slim as a dart, giving account of himself to his Honor. There was never any picture more to delight the heart of a painter. Douglas in high thick stockings reaching up to his thighs like leather leggings worn by those 16th-Century men, a tight fitting short fur-lined coat with wide fur collar closely turned up around his face, a close fitting tasseled cap was on his head and big fur gauntlets protected his hands. And there was Papa, looking almost slight beside the giant Governor, in his fur-lined coat of fine broadcloth and fur cap and gauntlets and snow white beard. Yes, he represented the rich courtly merchant prince; and there was the sparse figure of Maunsall, veteran soldier. Grouped around were other picturesque figures—Gardiner [son of Charles and Grace Bell] in Norfolk jacket close belted, gracefully skating back and forth; Casey in a fur coat and tasseled cap; other men in short fur or leather coats with high laced sealskin boots; and lithe active boys swiftly chasing the hockey puck while waiting until the young knight's conference with His Honor should be over and he would mount his very modern chariot and be off with them all tagging after him.[9]

The school children were given a holiday in honor of the lieutenant governor's visit, and they watched the flights from the ice on Baddeck Bay. One farmer had driven over fifteen miles with his horse and sleigh to be present. So intent did he become watching the flying machine soaring overhead that he failed to notice his horse had moved forward on the clampers of ice that filled the upper part of the bay. Suddenly his sleigh jerked forward and nothing was to be seen of the horse but its head. For a time there was great excitement until the man and his horse were rescued from the icy waters. Not only were the people fascinated by the flights; some seals, attracted by the engine and propeller noises, scrambled up on the ice in order to satisfy their curiosity.

It was noted in the *Beinn Bhreagh Recorder* that the lieutenant governor was very impressed by the achievements of Baldwin and McCurdy and spoke of the importance of the work they were doing:

"Why," said he, "just think of the different uses these machines could be put to if the Canadian Government owned them. Not only would they be important in time of war, but they could be used for the purpose of exploration in the far North where explorers encounter so many hardships and privations."[10]

In spite of the enthusiasm of the governor general and the lieutenant governor and a favorable report by Major Maunsall, the official attitude taken after the crash at Petawawa of the *Silver Dart* and the *Baddeck No. 1* remained unfavorable. The young company never succeeded in obtaining the government orders so essential for its existence. McCurdy (later the lieutenant governor of Nova Scotia) became the most successful aviator of the group, while Baldwin dropped out of active flying to concentrate on the theoretical aspects of flight. As for the fate of the *Baddeck No. 2*, Mrs. Baldwin said that she and Casey were unable to stand the sight of this historic plane rotting away on the beach at Baddeck, so one day, in desperation, they made a bonfire out of it.

In the late summer of 1910 Alec and Mabel went around the world accompanied by the Baldwins. By the following March Mabel began longing for home, as this letter to Elsie suggests:

I wish we could come straight home to you, but Papa and Casey want to stay for the Aviation Meet at Monaco on April 11th to have an opportunity of examining the motors and probably investing in one with which to make another attempt to fly his own machine [*Cygnet II*]. I do not feel I have the right to stand in their way and it is exactly the spur they need before beginning work again. I also think that perhaps a few days' rest on the Riviera is what we all need. You see I lost a lot of strength in India and even the week we had in Mentone did not quite set me up again, although it worked wonders.[11]

After returning from their world tour, Bell and Baldwin decided to apply some of the principles of powered flight to a water craft. The result was the hydrofoil hydrodrome boat commonly referred to as the H.D. They hoped to transport heavy loads at speed comparable to those attained by aircraft using air propellers for the driving force.

To overcome water resistance, a set of wing-like surfaces were attached to the sides of the hull below the waterline. Known as hydrofoils, they were arranged in vertical tiers, tapering toward the bottom. At high speed, the boat would rise on these hydrofoils until it rested on the smallest tier of foils, raising the entire hull above the water. Mabel was as interested in these experiments as she had been in the experiments with flying machines.

World War I broke out on August 4, 1914. In November of that year she wrote Daisy:

By the way, Papa is getting restive about the H.D. He believes it is ready to submit to Naval experts and it is in condition to demonstrate its possibilities if taken up and pushed. Casey does not believe that the Canadian Government would bother with it and will not bring it to their attention. Therefore, Papa wants to have one of our Navy experts sent up from Washington to look it over. Papa's point is that it is the fastest boat for the horsepower developed. Also, that it is the one boat that could today pass over the mine-infested harbor of Kiel or Heligoland, ram a German ironclad and come out again before anyone knew what had happened. There are motor boats of over 60 miles an hour, I believe, but they could not go over those mines for they require 1,500 horsepower to do what Casey's H.D. does with 100. Moreover, Casey's can stand weight without submersion and could be armored.[12]

Apart from their experimental work on the hydrodome, Bell and Baldwin built boats at Beinn Bhreagh for the Canadian Navy. Mabel's letters to Daisy gave a picture of life at Beinn Bhreagh during these war years:

Instead of the pretty rustic bridge are ugly boat sheds and machine shops. It is the price we must pay to stay here. Neither of my sons-in-law would care to live here and we could not stay ourselves without Casey. He too would not stay without work that seems to him worthwhile and it gives both Daddysan and me an interest that we need. Daddysan putters away but with-

out the energy and fire of youth he could not carry on the burden of the laboratory alone....[13]

I wish you and David were here to admire my garden. I am in the depths today. It is the most glorious day imaginable and my gardens are at the height of their beauty, full of weeds to be sure, but also a perfect riot of the most glorious flowers springing up naturally as of their own delight in life and there is nobody who cares. I could weep. Well, there are other things than flowers and I have spent hours of the time I would love to give to working over them this first year that my gardens are really mine, drying vegetables and each day learning that it not such a simple job as one might think or as easy.

Everyone here is anxious to see the process and I am to give a demonstration at the I.O.D.E. tearoom tomorrow. I feel less able than ever to tell them anything, as I find most every farmer's wife has dried things for years and has her own formula which is perfectly satisfactory. However, the fame of the dried spinach I served at Daddysan's "gig" dinner has spread all over the countryside. It was "perfectly delicious," report said, so all the wives want to see how I did it. I am scared of my reputation because I find that not every drying is a success. However, even the far-famed Mrs. Edward McCurdy "of German birth, poor thing, but all right nevertheless," only dries string beans, so there is hope for my spinach.[14]

While everyone at Beinn Bhreagh was involved in making their contribution to the war effort, Mabel could not hide her concern for the future:

I say to Daddysan, "But what will happen to us after the war is over and we are left with all this plant?" He replied, "Sufficient unto the day is the evil thereof." We have to do the best we can now and let tomorrow take care of itself. So we are hewing down cherished trees, destroying the best-loved beauty spots on Beinn Bhreagh and erecting in their place huge ugly sheds just in the hope that we may be allowed to build ships for the U.S. Government. We don't even know we will be allowed to do it, but Daddysan's orders are that no time is to be lost in waiting.

So it is one big gamble but our hopes are high, for Casey says we can do as good and as cheap a job as any except the biggest firms and it is not a question of money but time. Only so many people can work profitably at one boat. The fourteen gigs are beauties; two ride proudly at anchor. "Finished," yes, that is, finished all but the rudders. Four more are practically finished and the rest should be safely within the ninety days Casey allows of the hundred days the government gives for delivery FOB Halifax.[15]

The completion of this contract was celebrated by holding a dinner party at Beinn Bhreagh for the workmen. Mabel wrote to Daisy:

I may have time for a few words while the men are surrounding Daddysan at the piano singing the old, old songs, preparatory to "God Save the King" and "Goodnight." It is just twelve and thirty-eight people sat down to dinner at eight-thirty.

The table was set diagonally across the room, extending into the tower, and down the middle was first

203

my cheval glass and then my round bureau mirror. The two were banked with moss connected by a smaller mirror and there were little maple and fir and beech trees growing bending over the water. On the water [mirrors] was a long line of fourteen little silver boats, exact copies in silver paper of the fourteen beautiful boats that on Sunday lay strung out in a line from the *Cygnet* shed to the *Baddeck* shed. They really are awfully well done and were extremely neat, trim and good copies. Casey was delighted. Then there were the Allies' flags with a tiny English and American flag at each place and the name cards were photographs of the gigs taken Sunday morning. Well, as I said, they sat down at 8:30 and got up somewhere about 11:30 and apparently are still at the piano led by Daddysan. He is in high feather, looking his Santa Claus best in white waist coat and velvet coat and very much alive.

He made a long speech on his favorite themes, the laboratory boat building and our fastest motor boat in the world. At all events, he did make a good speech. I know because I peeked through a slat in the window shade and it just framed him as he stood talking with old-time energy and vim. He certainly is very well these days, although he also is not strong. Casey sat opposite and smoked his pipe. Our guests were the laboratory staff, twenty-five of them and some "city magnates," as Casey calls them and it was to celebrate the completion ten days ahead of time of our first government order.[16]

By expanding their boat building plant and investing in expensive equipment, Bell and Baldwin were confident that they could build the 110-foot submarine chasers required by the U.S. Naval Department. They offered their services, promising to deliver three such vessels in the spring of 1918. Indeed, so confident were they of getting the contract that they had begun clearing land for the enlarged sheds.

It came as a great blow to receive the following telegram from Gilbert Grosvenor:

The Government regrets that it cannot place an order for any boats for such late delivery as specified in your telegram. Conditions have materially changed during the past several days and no further orders are now being placed for these boats. Exceedingly regret outcome of this affair. Writing.[17]

Mabel wrote to Daisy:

I am flopped down—feel as if mourning over the loss of a dear friend. It really hurts and it is an effort just to write to you. We have been so wrought up, so exalted, with the idea of building these big ships and have gone ahead just as if it were a sure thing, in order to lose no time and now—Bert's [Grosvenor] telegram putting an end to everything. It's really the end of everything I am afraid. We may get small boats from Halifax but Casey won't stay for that. We were so full of enthusiasm, it is terrible now. It seemed as if we were really to do something big, now we can't. From the midst of life we are now in death—the death of all our hopes and high endeavors. For nothing have we killed our beautiful trees, destroyed the glory of the harbor. It was so worthwhile, any sacrifice was exalted in, now....[18]

In the spring of 1917 Mabel remained in Washington while Alec returned to Beinn Bhreagh. At first she felt very lonely and out of touch with the Washington scene and longed for Alec:

I do miss you so. The bottom has dropped out of my life and all purpose gone. Nobody wants me, perhaps it is a case of "I love nobody, no not I and nobody loves me!" For certainly with you for company, to plan for and take care of, I don't want anybody else very much; people realize that and I am left alone. We don't seem to be together very much do we, yet you are not out of my mind all day. I am either waiting for our morning chat together, our midday drive, our afternoon return home and our after-dinner movie with little time for anything else. Now all the time is my own and I don't know what to do with it. Or if I do, I don't want it, I just want you! Everyone seems to be going their own way, living their own lives in which I have no part or lot....[19]

I am getting nervous about you. It is such a long hard journey [from Washington to Beinn Bhreagh] and I am not there to look after you. I want you to come back for I feel that you need to keep in touch with things here for a little longer before we bury ourselves in the country.[20]

In March of 1917 the United States entered the war and Mabel was soon caught up in the excitement of it in Washington. When the bill authorizing universal military training came before Congress, she was inspired to write this appeal to the women of her country:

To the Women of America. Mothers, Wives and Daughters of Brave Men. Attention!

206

Your men are leaving you—flocking to join the colors. The President calls, our Country's honor, the Nation's safety demands the services of its citizens.

It is right that they go.

But is it right, is it just and equitable that they, the brave and patriotic should alone perform this duty—a duty which rests on all alike?

Everybody realizes how unfair it would be to let the government be run alone or chiefly by the voluntary contributions of the patriotic while the unpatriotic shared its benefits without paying.

But it is not so clearly perceived that to place the burden of its defense alone or in a large degree on patriotic volunteers is the same in principle. It makes the patriotic suffer for the unpatriotic.

Universal Military Training is a means whereby the whole citizenship of the nation can be made to contribute to its maintenance.

You should not try to prevent your boys from springing to their country's aid, but you should have the right to insist that they shall not be left alone to bear the brunt, that they shall not be sacrificed for the unpatriotic.

If you want to save them, you must act now, at once without a moment's delay. The Bill authorizing the Universal Military Training is now before Congress. The forces arrayed against it are united and powerful; remember what is at stake. Your men's chances of returning to you are lessened if the Bill fails to pass for they will have to do double duty.

What you have to do is to telegraph at once your

Congressman. Tell your neighbors about it and get them to act too. Show them you ask for nothing but justice, for the principle that as all contribute to the maintenance of the government, so must all contribute to its defense. And act now. Tomorrow may be too late.[21]

Bert Grosvenor showed Mabel's appeal for conscription to U.S. Secretary of the Interior Franklin Knight. He thought the argument sound and recommended it be printed by the Naval Department. More than 2,500 copies were sent out, all signed by Mabel. She confided to Alec, enjoying the excitement of being personally involved:

It just breaks my heart to think you are not here these last few weeks to meet all these interesting foreignors. I have had two or three charming notes sent to me by Mr. Balfour [Britain's prime minister from 1902-1905 who was over from London] and have met two charming French aviators and missed the chance of seeing others all because you weren't there.

Then there is all the Department activity that I have come in for through Bert and David and I am afraid it will seem a sort of backwater in Baddeck except that it is never so where you are. Well, I have so many irons on the fire I shall just have to leave them to fizzle themselves out when I go to you.[22]

Mabel realized that the two most important things for the war effort were to stop enemy submarines and to raise food for the Allies. When she returned to Beinn Bhreagh she convinced Alec and Casey Baldwin that the world needed the hydrodome as a submarine chaser.

Although the outstanding record of the H.D.-4 aroused great interest in naval circles, the faith that both

Baldwin and the Bells had in their hydrofoil craft was not shared by the Canadian, British or American governments. Perhaps because of indifference or lack of courage, the Canadians preferred to continue in their usual role as producers of raw materials for manufacture elsewhere and as a market for manufactured goods. Without government contracts the company, Bell-Baldwin Hydrodromes Limited, was unable to function and by March 31, 1923, it had ceased to exist.[23]

17
A Forgotten Page of History

Alec's indifference to public recognition of his inventive genius was always a matter of concern to Mabel. She wanted him recognized not only by his scientific associates, but also by the world at large. In this respect she was frequently frustrated by him, as she confided to Daisy:

I never saw anybody who threw his whole body and mind and heart into all that interested him in a hundred different directions, like the waves beating on the shore fling seaweed on the sand and then retreat to fling more seaweed in some other wildly separated place. Papa flings ideas, suggestions, accomplishments upon all recklessly and leaves them lying there to ferti-

lize other minds, instead of gathering them all together to form creations to his own honor and glory.[1]

Bell spent years of his life defending his telephone patents in the courts, but at heart he did not feel that his claim as the inventor was the important thing; his interest lay in solving the problem. Later in life, with his reputation as an inventor firmly established, he often thrust the credit for an invention on his associates. He always referred to the hydrodrome as "Mr. Baldwin's invention." This distressed Casey so much that he complained to Mabel that he could not continue working on it unless Bell shared in the credit. Mabel tried to soothe him, but when Bell wrote to the same effect in the *A.E.A. Bulletin*, Mabel felt that he'd gone too far and wrote to Daisy and David Fairchild:

Daddysan makes me mad, he will pile credit on other people vicariously. I am perfectly devoted to Casey as you know and most certainly want him to have all the credit he deserves, and that is a lot. But Father is working on the *Dhonnas Beag* [H.D.-1] too, and no step is made without him. It is not fair for Father to report in the *Bulletin* that "Mr. Baldwin proposes to do so and so," just as if Casey were moving entirely independent of him, which he certainly is not. Casey is superintending and pushing the experiments on the *Dhonnas Beag* and he is intensely interested and a lot of credit is due him. Father would not have carried out those experiments at this time but for him. It was he who got Father to let him go ahead and try them while we were waiting for favorable breezes. He is doing the work—but Father is as much interested as he—and has had the same idea of the possibilities of this method

of rising from the water—he meant to make the experiment himself whenever he got time. Casey is doing it all for him after talking over everything with him. My point is that this work is conjointly Daddysan's and Casey's—while from what Daddysan has written, one would think it was Casey's solely and absolutely.

Father did the same thing about the Hammondsport aerodromes. The *Red Wing, White Wing, June Bug* and the *Silver Dart* were all the collective product of all the A.E.A. associates working as an Association. The *Red Wing* was, as Daddy expressed it, "constructed according to plans approved by Liet. Selfridge," which was true as far as it went, but as a matter of fact the idea of putting it on skids to run on the ice was (I think) Casey's and the trussing employed was of his devising. On the *Red Wing* there [were] no adjustable tips—[these were] added to the *White Wing* after a suggestion contained in a letter written to Casey by Daddysan—these tips are one of the most important features the *White Wing, June Bug* and *Silver Dart* possess. Father also contributed several other very important ideas regarding the steering gear, etc. So that while the *White Wing* was approved by Casey, the *June Bug* by Curtiss, the *Silver Dart* by Douglas, as a matter of fact they are all the work of the whole Association including Daddysan, and Daddysan's work certainly was quite as important in the original features as any, to say the least.

I am writing all this to you and David on purpose because this is history and I want it to go on record—so please keep this letter. I might appeal to Casey to correct Papa's report, but I don't want to do that because it would only make him uncomfortable and might make him hesitate to go on. There was never anyone more regardless of self in these matters than Casey. He simply wants to get things done and he wants to push them through with all his might, regardless of whose the idea originally was. If it appeals to his judgment, he will work at it and will never lift a finger if some other fellow claims credit for the idea. I am the only selfish person in the Trinity, but I like to have things fair. I want Casey given every credit for independent ideas and for the energy in carrying it out and pushing it to completion. Many of the engineering details are of his sole devising. Father expressed it correctly in the beginning, "he turned over this branch of the problem," that is right—but this does not mean that he himself had not thought it all out in gross. Casey had received the idea—worked out by Daddy-san and himself—and is trying to work it out practically—and is personally superintending every detail. He is the author and inventor of many devices—but Father has helped him with valuable suggestions also—so that the work is not solely Casey's. That's all.[2]

Daisy recalled that her father and mother only looked for the best in people, and her father wouldn't tolerate the least disparagement of anyone. Although her mother didn't carry this kindly point of view to the lengths that her father did, she admired his principles and respected his wishes. This may account for the fact that neither the Grosvenors nor the Fairchilds were aware of Curtiss's relationship, in after years, with the other members of the Aerial Experiment Association. Both families were upset because Casey Baldwin made no attempt to obtain any financial benefit from the H.D.-4, which had already achieved a world record for speed. In 1919 David Fairchild wrote to his father- and mother-in-law criticizing Baldwin severely for this lack of business acumen. Mabel came strongly to his defense:

I feel sure from the tone of some of your recent letters to Daddysan and me that you really know very little about Mr. Curtiss's relations to the old Aerial Experiment Association, that I feel I want to tell you something about them and the reasons why we cannot give him either respect or friendship.

I would not feel so concerned about your evident appreciation of him as a successful man who has made aeroplanes and millions while we others have dropped out, did it not also involve deprecation of others, which does them injustice. This hurts me dreadfully because I care so very much for your and Daisy's good opinion.

The Aerial Experiment Association was a great, a marvelous success yet very few know this; fewer still the magnitude of that success.

It accomplished what it set out to do—evolve a practical type of flying-machine—a type so remarkably perfect that all progress since has lain in details adapting it to the various uses to which it has been put—and in the improvement of the motive power.

A.E.A. machines not only won the Scientific American prize in 1908 and the International prize in France the next year, but they are the only type of biplanes successfully flying today. This is the type with which the wonderful aerial biplane battles have been

fought over the battlefields of the Great War. French, English, German, Italian—all are typical Aerial Experiment Association machines.

This is because the Aerial Experiment associates were the first of all men to discover, describe and apply the fundamental principles underlying all really practical biplane construction. The Wrights did not. Their type, as well as all others, have been discarded for ours. Curtiss, who knew every secret of the A.E.A., tried to find other methods and failed utterly. He changed a few unessential details but his claim of having got around our principles had no more justification than would an assertion that putting the Bell Receiver in a slightly different holder made it no longer a Bell Receiver. Those biplanes you saw flying overhead and thought of as Curtiss biplanes are not really Curtiss biplanes at all, they are Baldwin biplanes constructed on A.E.A. principles, just as are every other biplane now flying.

The world does not know this—but Curtiss does, and it is due to him that the world does not.... The other associates were mere enthusiastic boys, totally inexperienced in business, absolutely trustful of him. They were full of eagerness, fresh from college, but with no definite plans or prospects.

None of them, or Mr. Bell either, could have conceived that Curtiss was already scheming to betray them all in such a way as to make it practically impossible for them to reap their fair share of their mutual labors.

After the Association dissolved, Casey and Douglas were thrown out of work. The machines they had helped to create were sufficiently perfected. To go on tinkering with them would have been a waste of money. Patents had been applied for, but until they were granted, there was a scant hope of their getting a hearing from ordinary businessmen....

Very different was Glenn Curtiss's position. The close of the Association found him in sole possession of its workshop, which had been especially equipped for the making of aeroplanes; with men trained to the work and all the expensive, unprofitable, but absolutely necessary, preliminary experimental work done, and without cost to himself, and by trained mechanical engineers, whose services he could never alone have obtained. No other firm in the country, except perhaps the Wrights, was in such a favorable position to grasp the great opportunity to inaugurate a new business with immense possibilities.

He owed his introduction to the A.E.A. to his own energy and enterprise in having the fastest and lightest going motor then known in America. But the equipping of his shop, the training of his men and the doing of the experimental work he owed to my money, Mr. Bell's brains, and those of the other associates—all unobtainable otherwise. Curtiss himself had contributed little of value, apart from the fitting of his motor, to the development of the aeroplanes. Indeed it was not he, but Herring, who designed the camouflaged A.E.A. machine in which he later won the International prize....

Casey departed with us. Douglas, helped once more by Mr. Bell, struggled alone for awhile but dis-

215

credited by Curtiss accomplished nothing and finally was glad to accept a position with Curtiss as pilot—a position that acknowledged in no way his former equality with Curtiss....

Well, the years passed. Curtiss having squeezed Herring dry, tried to throw him off also but is now defendant in a suit Herring has brought with good chance of winning. By various means—wrecking one of his companies for instance, so that the Wrights could not collect on his infringement of their royalties—royalties which he would not have had to pay, had he stood squarely on our patents—Curtiss has amassed millions—and the rest of us have had to accept—almost as a gratuity—a few thousands and stock in a questionable company; and to share this little with Curtiss too!...

In 1917 as in 1878, men who could invent things people wanted were opposed by men, strong and unscrupulous who knew better how to sell them. The vital difference was Gardiner G. Hubbard. But for him, Mr. Bell probably would have been put off with a few thousands. Had a man like Mr. Hubbard, a born promoter—developer would be the truer word—been on our side in 1917, things might have been different now. Certainly he would not have yielded without a struggle as was done....

Glenn Curtiss stands before the public, a conspicuous figure, a millionaire, a successful man, who has developed a wonderful new industry. Casey Baldwin does not. Mr. Bell's name is rarely mentioned in connection with Aviation....

Now, once again Graham Bell and Casey Baldwin have something to offer the world.

As you say, just now the wonders of flying a hundred or two hundred miles in the air and of crossing the Atlantic in an air machine, appeals more to the imagination than just skimming the surface of the water a paltry seventy or eighty miles an hour, but even these amazing feats will pall as they become the commonplaces of every day and the water highway will resume interest.

So the question I am asking today is: "Must the experience of the A.E.A. be repeated, or is there any way by which some honor and pecuniary reward may be assured to those who have rightfully earned them?" Casey is much more alive to the desirability of getting something in return for our expenditures than he was, chiefly for Mr. Bell's and my sakes. But how? He needs help. It is no use saying he should come down and compete—he cannot do that. What I am looking for is someone who is willing to be the leader of a forlorn hope, for this is about the size of our job. Nevertheless, it is a big undertaking, worth a big man's best efforts and full of big possibilities. Nothing less in fact than the attempt to revolutionize our age-long methods of water travel.

Where shall I find him? I feel I have set myself a job on the face of it as absurd as the mouse's offer to help the lion. But she succeeded! Any suggestions thankfully received.[3]

In his biography *Glenn Curtiss: Pioneer of Flight*, Cecil Roseberry gives a detailed account of the Aerial Experiment Association and Curtiss's relationship with the various members of that association. He also traces the development of the many companies Curtiss controlled for the manufacturing of aeroplanes in the United States and tells of the bitter litigation instigated against Curtiss by Herring and the Wright Brothers. There is little, if anything, in Mabel Bell's letter that has not been corroborated by Curtiss's biographer.

The Fairchild and Grosvenor families were unable to respond to her plea for help. Realizing their limitations and the need of sound legal and business guidance, Casey, with Bell's agreement, enlisted the help of his brother-in-law Colonel John F. Lash, an able corporate lawyer from Toronto. Bell thought that they should try to reach some understanding with Forlanini, an Italian, and the three Americans, Dr. Peter Cooper-Hewitt, W.M. Meacham and L.E. Meacham, whose patents dealt with features similar to those contained in the Bell-Baldwin patents.

After protracted negotiations Colonel Lash and Casey ultimately did succeed in acquiring the Forlanini and Cooper-Hewitt patents and in reaching a working agreement with the Meachams. When Bell-Baldwin Hydrodromes Limited was formed on June 26, 1920, Colonel Lash served as its president.[4] But although Colonel Lash was an able legal attorney, he was not a developer in the sense that Gardiner G. Hubbard had been, and Mabel's estimation of Casey's business acumen proved to be all too correct. When the company ceased operations in 1923, the shell of the fantastic H.D.-4—fifty years ahead of its time—was left to rot on the shore below Beinn Bhreagh.

In the 1970s the craft, its back broken in two, was

hauled from the beach to a shed at the Alexander Graham Bell Museum and protected from the elements until the Alexander Graham Bell Complex was completed in 1978. The craft whose speed defied challengers for a decade is now on permanent display and serves as a belated tribute to the genius of the men who developed the hydrofoil concept.

18
Mabel's Grandchildren & the Montessori System

After Elsie and Daisy were married a new generation of children entered Mabel's life. Elsie and Gilbert Grosvenor had seven children, one of whom had died at the age of five. Daisy and David Fairchild had three; their oldest, a son, bore his grandfather's full name. Mabel loved tiny babies and nothing gave her greater pleasure than to hold them in her arms. She wrote how she felt about her first grandson:

Bert expects to be away from Beinn Bhreagh for ten days when Melville [Grosvenor] belongs practically to me. You never saw such a fascinating baby. I don't know how I lived without him from day to day. He is much more satisfactory than his mother was— poor little girlie.[1]

During the summer of 1905 Alec's father Melville Bell became dangerously ill and was brought from his summer home to Washington. Alec and Mabel nursed him through his last illness. Elsie and Bert were spending the summer at Beinn Bhreagh; Elsie had just given birth to Mabel, her third child. Mabel senior wrote Bert:

How I wish I could hold my baby [little Mabel] in my arms. Now you and Elsie must promise I can have this baby as I did Melville. Surely you don't think I did him any harm. Gertrude is exquisite but I always felt such a sense of loss that I, her own grandmother, wasn't allowed to share in the love she gave her nurse. A baby is a baby such a short time—but a year.[2]

When Daisy was expecting her first child in the summer of 1906, she hurried from her Maryland home in the country so the baby could be born in her father's study at 1331 Connecticut Avenue. Mabel was at Beinn Bhreagh. As soon as she heard the news, she left for Washington to be with her daughter, and from there wrote Alec:

The baby is to be scientifically brought up, so can't be coddled when he cries, which may be all right for the youngster but is hard on his grandmother. Mama [Mrs. Hubbard] was disappointed that the baby was not born at Twin Oaks but I fancy Daisy was afraid of the disapproval of the family if she inflicted more illness on Mama and so she came here.

How do you like the idea of this little baby's life beginning there among all your books in the room where so many brain babies of yours have been born? Do you suppose there are any germs floating around there which emanating from your brain will take root in the sensitive baby brain and come forth in later years?[3]

Each year the Grosvenor family made the long trip

from Washington to Beinn Bhreagh, making their home at the Lodge for the summer. The Fairchild family came often as well, staying with the Bells at Beinn Bhreagh Hall. Mabel wrote to David Fairchild:

I think these family gatherings here at Beinn Bhreagh where brothers and sisters and cousins meet together on equal terms in the old home with parents and grandparents are of great value. You who have lived together here, bound by common ties, can never in afterlife quite lose the affection and interest in each other which these visits foster. I was so pleased when Elsie told me that when she admonished her girls to remember that they were our visitors, they all rebelled and said, "they weren't visitors, they were at home."[4]

In 1914, when Melville Grosvenor was twelve years old, his parents left him in the care of his grandfather Bell when they returned to Washington. Mabel wrote to Bert:

I am almost jealous of the attention Mr. Bell is giving Melville. He did not devote himself so regularly to his own daughters but he says there is a difference—Melville is a boy. I wonder what would have happened if his own boys had lived.

I wonder if you realize how deeply I am interested in my grandchildren, particularly my grandsons. All the plans, the hopes and the ambitions that have laid buried in the graves of my own little sons sprang to life with the coming of each of my three grandsons.

You and Elsie, Daisy and David, may reasonably hope to see the coming of another generation of your own blood and in them continue whatever hopes you cherish for your own children. But these boys of yours

and David's are all in whom I can have an active personal interest. Therefore, I hope you will forgive me if sometimes I seem unduly meddlesome offering suggestions that occur to me of ways of helping them.[5]

A letter written to Elsie is full of such suggestions:

I wouldn't interfere with Gertrude's schooling if I were you. After all everybody has to fight the battles of life and I don't believe it is true kindness to try to make things too easy for one's children for it unfits them for competition with their fellows. It isn't simply fighting for one's daily bread. It is fighting for everything one wants, social position, love of one's fellows, everything that makes life worth living. Instead of trying to ease Gertrude's school work, I'd try to help her along some other way; don't let her do less work than her school fellows. I don't believe the spirit evolved by such indulgence would be good for her.[6]

Mabel had the greatest respect and admiration for her son-in-law, David Fairchild. She was pleased and flattered that he enjoyed discussing all sorts of subjects with her, but the quality of his scientific mind had an abrasive effect on her that was entirely lacking in the relationship with her other son-in-law. Just as she had wanted her daughters to have as wide an experience of life as possible, she tried now to do the same for her grandchildren and did not take kindly to being frustrated in her attempts. She wrote to David:

Elsie and Bert say they have tried to persuade you to let Graham come up [to Beinn Bhreagh] but you objected from some idea that he might "get out of hand." Elsie said she couldn't exactly explain but that her idea was that you had some feeling that Graham should be "hardened."

My feeling is that you have some sort of moral idea that Graham should be taught the virtue of renunciation, the delight (?) of doing without something he wanted, of denial of luxury; I am sure some such thought is in the back of your mind—has been there for years—and so you know both Mr. Bell and I dread the result of it on Graham. Don't you know how often it happens that clergymen's sons turn out wild because of the restraint of their early days? I cannot believe it can hurt a boy who must anyway earn his own living to have a carefree, happy boyhood with all the luxury attainable thrown in. It all makes a wonderful memory for after years. I well remember the joy of my own childhood, rides in my grandmother's crimson satin glass coach with the stately and very cross Patrick perched on high behind his gray horses. I never expected to attain such grandeur, my own home was much simpler, but I thoroughly enjoyed it and it never spoilt my own home.

But all this is general principles. The reason I wish so much that this particular grandchild of ours should be here this summer [1917] is that he will be in surroundings and subject to influences that never again can be his. Daddysan, up to quite lately, has been remarkably well, and I hope he will be so again, I want your gifted boy to know him while he is still bright and full of mental vigor, and he has been so to an unusual degree this summer.

Then this war excitement has struck us with

wonderful force and you would not know the place. Bobby's [Baldwin] nursery is now Casey's office. Here Casey works nearly all day and night, except when he is superintending the work of the shops. The spirit is wonderful. Bert appears amazed at what is being accomplished; the two lifeboats being built in two weeks are wonderful affairs, and the men work with absorption and earnestness that would astonish you. He, I think, always felt there was not enough of this.

There are now twenty-five men at work and in a few days there will probably be several more, and they work eleven hours instead of nine. Of course they are paid, but it is not this that moves them. It is the thought that they, too, are soldiers of Canada working in their way for the cause of liberty.

I want Graham to get this view of a new side of life while it is in its first freshness. Surely you have not forgotten how Hammondsport impressed you. This is Graham's chance to experience the thrill and wonder of it. I cannot see why it should hurt the future biologist to know that this is not the whole of life. It seems to me it cannot but be a broadening influence; I cannot see how a month of it could allow him to get permanently "out of hand." If it does, it will simply show that he never was really in hand at all. Life is going to tame him soon enough. Let him go to some working place later when this is no longer open to him—that time will come soon enough, never fear. He is just at the age when he can appreciate what he sees.[7]

When Graham Fairchild was a little boy Mabel was anxious that he should attend a good kindergarten. She made a point of visiting all those available in the vicinity of Washington, but was far from satisfied with what she found. About this time she read a fascinating account of the life of Dr. Maria Montessori and her amazing achievement in devising a new system of education for young children living in the slums of Rome.

Born in 1870, Maria Montessori was twelve years old when her parents moved to Rome to give their only child a better education than what was available in their native province of Ancona. At first Maria became interested in engineering and attended a technical school for boys. Then her taste changed and she became more interested in biology. She attended the medical school connected with the University of Rome and in 1894, after great difficulties, became the first woman to receive a medical degree in Italy. For the next decade she engaged in various medical and educational pursuits. She was an assistant director of the university's psychiatric clinic, a lecturer in anthropology, a teacher of deficient children and a trainer of teachers.

In 1906 Montessori was known only within her immediate circle. Two years later her name had become known throughout the world. In that short time she had made the discovery for which all her previous life had been a preparation—she discovered the life within the child.

There existed in Rome at the time a slum area known as the San Lorenzo quarter. The Instituto Romano dei Stabili, a building society, erected two large blocks of flats in this district housing about a thousand poor people. Most of the parents worked during the day, leaving their small children to their own devices, and as a result much damage was done to the buildings. Instead of repainting and repairing at

225

frequent intervals, the owners decided to set aside a room and employ someone to take care of the children. Dr. Montessori was asked to direct this undertaking.

Montessori believed that methods that had proved so successful with backward children would be equally successful with normal children. She didn't look after the children herself, but supervised another woman in the first Casa dei Bambini, or "Home for Children," as the American writer Dorothy Canfield Fisher translated the term.

Montessori discovered that these children had amazing powers of concentration; they loved doing this over and over again, and came to prefer work to play. In no time at all they acquired a sense of personal dignity, and before long were anxious to express themselves by writing.

Miss Anne E. George, a primary school teacher in Chicago concerned about the quality of education American children were receiving, learned of Dr. Montessori's achievement. She went to Rome to study her methods. Upon her return to the United States in 1911, she established a school at Tarrytown, New York, based on the Montessori system. Miss Roberta Fletcher, also trained in Rome, assisted her.

Mabel read about this school and went to Tarrytown to see it for herself. So impressed was she that she persuaded Miss Fletcher to come to Beinn Bhreagh for the summer of 1912 and conduct a school there for her grandchildren and some of the local youngsters. This was the first Montessori school in Canada and the second on the American continent.

When they returned to Washington in October, a larger school was opened in the annex of the Bell home for the grandchildren and their little friends. The school-room was furnished with low tables and chairs and plenty of shelves for the specially designed teaching material. The floor was covered with small scattered rugs that the children were free to move about. Unlike most school-rooms, this one had a piano. Twenty-three children were enrolled that first year.

In April 1913, over two hundred and fifty interested people gathered in the Bell home, and from among them a committee was formed to establish a permanent Montessori school in Washington under the direction of Miss George and Miss Fletcher. Committee members scoured the city searching for a suitable location for the school. When they found a large old house and garden at 1840 Kalorama Road, Mabel bought it and arranged the necessary renovations before renting it to the committee.

At a second meeting in the Bell home, the Montessori Educational Association was organized with Mabel appointed president and Miss Margaret Wilson, daughter of President Woodrow Wilson, on the Board of Trustees. The association's purpose was to help establish Montessori schools across the country. Members felt that an educational movement of great magnitude and importance had been started, and that the Montessori principles of education would spread from Washington as a center to all parts of the United States.

The association invited Dr. Montessori to visit America. She came in 1914. Samuel McClure, editor of *McClure's Magazine*, who had visited her school in Rome, organized a successful speaking tour. The opening lecture was given in Washington with Alexander Bell presiding. Dr. Montessori began with a cordial appreciation of her reception in America and a charming reference to Mrs. Bell declaring that she "had taken this method in her arms as a mother would take a child."[8]

Mabel wrote a letter to Mrs. Kennan in which she told her of her interest in the Montessori system of education and concluded:

I want my grandchildren to be workers and if the Montessori System does not make them efficient men and women, looking on work as the noblest thing of all, I shall be disappointed.[9]

For the next several years the outburst of enthusiasm for the Montessori method continued to spread across the United States. Then it died out almost as quickly as it had started. There were a number of reasons for this change of attitude. Most of the Montessori system's support had come from elite political and educational progressives and through such popular magazines as *McClure's*, not from those formulating the psychological theories and philosophy of education. In 1914 Professor William Kilpatrick's book *Montessori System Examined* was critical of the concept. As a respected professor at Teachers' College, Columbia University, he had a tremendous influence on professional educators, and his book dampened enthusiasm for the Montessori method.

This change of public attitude had little effect on Mabel's respect for the system, and for a number of years the Kalorama Road School continued to absorb her interest. Gradually, more and more of the financial responsibility for finding trained teachers and maintaining the school fell on her shoulders.

During the war years it was no longer feasible for Americans to train under Dr. Montessori in Rome. Unfortunately, no training center had been established in North America. As the trained teachers in the Kalorama School became involved with the war effort, it became impossible to replace them. Reluctantly, in 1919, Mabel closed the school.

19
Life in Retrospect

During the last few years of her life, Mabel spent more and more time with her husband at Beinn Bhreagh without the usual host of visitors; this gave her time to reflect upon her own life. She often shared these thoughts with her sons-in-law, who were both very close to her. She wrote to David Fairchild:

I feel the great mistake of my life has been the surrendering of myself too much to people who happened to be about me. I have always felt as if I were living on a moving train with no abiding home anywhere. I am always in such a rush preparing a winter or summer resort for other people that I have never had time to feel at home and settled in my own house myself. It is a great pleasure to me to step into Kathleen's [Baldwin] little home as I do every day at the end of my walk with Father and find her quietly and happily at work

at something in her own home with her husband [Casey] constantly in and out about his business. Sometimes she is at the piano singing away, sometimes busy on a Club paper, more often "fussing" about her house, arranging and rearranging her things.

Well, how one's pen does run away with one when it works as smoothly as now. I never meant to say all this about Kathleen, it is only that seeing her so homelike and happy, and seeing Mrs. Mills [the gardener's wife] too so homelike and happy in her even tinier and very humble home, makes me feel as if somehow I have never taught my own children what the ideal home should be. I am a "woman suffragist," to this extent that I think that as the State is made up of women as well as men, they should have equal say in the making of laws that govern them as well as men. The State, in the last analysis, is but the enlargement of the family. Formerly the husband was also the master of his wife, now the wife has entered into the partnership with the husband and they work together for the interests of the home. So I think women should have a partnership with men in the government of the State.[1]

There existed between Mabel and her son-in-law Bert Grosvenor a deep love, mutual respect and understanding. Mabel's long-standing interest and concern for the well-being of the National Geographic Society was a bond between them. Possibly not even Elsie shared the satisfaction that Mabel did in Bert's outstanding success as editor of the National Geographic Society's magazine and his achievement in making the society so influential in the scientific world. It was perhaps easier for her to discuss those things that lay closest to her heart with Bert than it was with any other family member:

In any crisis I want no other help than that which Mr. Bell always gives me. I am absolutely sure he will give up everything to stand by me and support me in every way. But the crisis over—I must just go my own daily way alone. He has never since we were married bestowed on me the constant instinctive thoughtful little attentions that you are always paying Elsie. From the very first year I found that he would go his own way. To try and appeal to him to go to bed because I was tired was no use. He would come when he had finished that interesting experiment or book and that might not be for hours. In short, to look for consideration from him in little everyday things was just like batting against a stone wall. Sometimes I try even now, it's no use unless it runs with his own convenience. So I know it is just this way with my husband.

I am sure of his absolutely unselfish devotion when he sees I am in an emergency and he will mean to be lovely all the time, but he just gets so interested in what he is doing that he simply can't tear himself away. Now you have married his daughter and Elsie is very like him. I can't imagine being the wife of anyone else. I have never coveted anybody else's husband instead of my own. Yet there have been times when I would have liked him to think of me the way you think of Elsie and we have had our tiffs all right. But on the whole, I learned early what I could expect from my husband and what I must do without or get elsewhere.[2]

Bert did not hesitate to discuss his wife with her

mother for he was sure of Mabel's help and understanding, as expressed in her letter to him:

I wish I could help you to interest Elsie in her garden. I think like you that it would be a great thing for her if she were interested but I don't really know how to bring it about.

I never tried harder than to interest Elsie in things Florentine and Japanese and in nothing else did I fail more conspicuously, so now I am afraid to try.

I really think Elsie is of too strong and distinct a personality to be persuaded into anything that does not match with her own instincts. In this she is like her father. He had always allowed me to do exactly as I pleased but he has never had more than a very lukewarm interest in my painting for example. I was trained to be an artist and might have done fairly well if he had cared. In the same way he never had more than a general interest in my garden. But he has been really interested in my Baddeck Club and in the Baddeck Public Library and also in the Montessori organization and it is really because of his enthusiasm that I have gone on with them. Now in these three last things there was executive and social work to be done, which he could and did do with great ability and enjoyment.[3]

In November 1915 Gilbert Grosvenor organized a testimonial dinner on behalf of the National Geographic Society to honor Colonel John J. Carty, and he asked Bell to propose the toast. Colonel Carty, a distinguished scientist and engineer, devoted his life to furthering the development of the telephone. He served in various positions with the American Telephone Company, including that of chief engineer. He reorganized and consolidated the company's experimental laboratories in Boston, New York, Chicago and elsewhere into the Bell Telephone Laboratory in New York, and was instrumental in overcoming the problems of long-distance telephone communication. As a result of his efforts, the New York-San Francisco line was opened to public service on January 25, 1915. This achievement was further extended when on October 21 of the same year the human voice was transmitted for the first time across the Atlantic, a feat accomplished by radio telephone from the U.S. naval station at Arlington, Virginia, to the Eiffel Tower in Paris.

Mabel was delighted that her husband should be asked to propose this toast, for as always she was anxious that the world should know of the achievements of Alexander Graham Bell and publicly appreciate them. She saw immediately how this honor could rebound to her husband's glory:

It seems to me just celebrating an anniversary is just marking time—it is celebrating a thing that is past and in a way consigns Father to the long past also. It does not bring clearly before the public imagination the fact that he really belongs to the present and the future. That it is his work that is going on and on.

By celebrating Mr. Carty's feat and making Father the one to toast him, you put him in the position of the master honoring his disciple, who has just carried his own work to the furthest point yet reached. Isn't this the most dramatic thing possible? Doesn't this bring the bigness, the marvel of what Father has accomplished forty years ago much more forcibly home

to the public imagination than any mere celebration of a historical event?

The telephone in all its forms, its manifold usefulness, is more than ever to the fore today. This is above all things a Telephone War [1914-1918]. Everybody realized this more or less but that it is Alexander Graham Bell's invention that is doing the work does not occur to many minds. His name was not ever prominently mentioned in the public dispatches announcing the successful attempt to speak round the globe without wires. If any one man was thought of in this connection it was probably Marconi. By bringing Father and Carty together before the public, you do make Father's intimate connection with this great present wonder clear. And while Carty is officially honored, Father looms the biggest and those who are capable of appreciating it are thrilled by the wonder and splendor of it and what he did.

Can't you see what a great service you will be rendering Father and in a way so indirect that even he will not be embarrassed?[4]

As an editor, Bert was fascinated by Bell's life and the story of the invention of the telephone. As early as 1906 he was proposing to write a historical novel on the subject, but it never materialized. Over the years he continued to gather biographical material on Bell, and the proposed biography was a frequent subject of many of the letters that Mabel and Bert exchanged with each other. As the years went by, it became a matter of great importance to Mabel:

I told you frankly this morning how I feel about having a member of the family do the actual writing of the biography but I really don't mean to impose my opinions on the family. It is simply that I think the position I take is the sound one, that is all. I feel that the Alexander Graham Bell that I see must be very different from the Alexander Graham Bell outsiders see.

I see no reason why I should not tell the world what I think of him if I want to, nor do I see any reason why you or anybody else should not do the same, but it does seem to me that if a regular biography is ever written, it should be by one at a greater distance, and not by a woman. I think it takes a man to understand a man and a woman to appreciate a woman.

I think it would be very nice if Mabel [Bert's daughter] were interested to work with you on it. And I do think it very nice of you to be so much interested in the matter. I am a horrid cold thing but my husband is so much to me that I know the very best account that could be written will seem to me wrong in some way. It would praise him perhaps, but in ways that did not seem to me true and I would hate to have things attributed to him that were not so. He is big enough to stand as he is, a man, very imperfect, lacking in things that are lovely in other men, but a big good man all the same. Broad-minded, generous and tolerant in some things beyond the comprehension of most and then curiously the opposite in other things. I do not know a person with whom he has not fought at some time or other. Sometimes his wife has thought him badly in the wrong and at other times, entirely in the right. I could never say this publicly, and none of us would either, which would mean that the book would be inadequate.

Please forgive me and remember the whole thing touches me in my tenderest part and I can't be as nice about it as I would if I didn't care so much.[5]

Of all the letters Mabel wrote to her son-in-law, perhaps the most revealing was the one in which she enlisted his support for the Clarke School for the Deaf:

I am sending enclosed a copy of a letter I have written as I think it will give you and Elsie and indeed all the family a new point of view.

There is one thing I have always put aside because its acceptance involved the acceptance of things which have been my life-long desire to forget or at least ignore—the fact that I am not quite as other people. I have never been proud of the fact that although totally without hearing I have been able to mix with normal people. Instead, I have striven in every possible way to have that fact forgotten and so to appear so completely normal that I would pass as one. To have anything to do with other deaf people instantly brought the hardly concealed fact into evidence. So I have helped other things and other people—Montessori, Arts and Crafts, war suffering, anything and everything but the deaf. My deaf cousins were never invited to a dinner party. To say a child was deaf was enough to make me refuse to take any public notice of it. If help had to be given, it was always given at a distance. Of all people I hated most was a teacher of the deaf. I was always on the lookout for a little difference in their manner of addressing me, which would reveal the fact that I was a "case" in their eyes.

When my girls were young, I was particularly

236

careful to keep them away from association—and therefore possible interest and sympathy—with the deaf. Above all things I was antagonistic to my husband's efforts to keep up his association with the deaf and to continue his teaching of them.

Well this is a confession of great selfishness on my part. The only excuse I can offer is that it is just the spirit enlightened teachers of the deaf wish to see manifested in their pupils. They don't want them to band together and become "a peculiar people." My husband was in entire sympathy with my wish to keep our daughters away from contact with other deaf people whom they might possibly want to marry.

I think most people with a serious defect would sympathize with me. I don't think a man with a club foot wants to parade it in public. Two with the same defect emphasize each other, one alone might escape notice but not two together. I have never been able to understand why Cousin Lena likes to go shopping with me. To me it is perfectly awful when a shopgirl turns in perplexity and a little shrinking—oh I have seen it so many times—to me, and I have only made matters worse. When I was young and struggling for a foothold in society of my natural equals, I could not be nice to other deaf people. It was a case of self-preservation.

Now that I have made the situation clear to you, you will understand when I say if I were still a young woman with social aspirations or with daughters of marriageable age, I could not identify myself with the Clarke School for the Deaf. But that stage is passed and I have now awakened to a realization that I have not done my duty by the memory of the wonderful father and mother who not only did much for their child but so unselfishly labored for the benefit of other deaf children. Clarke School is their greatest and noblest monument and no one, not even their descendants, know it. They allowed others to carry off the credit: Clarke's name the school bears, Dudley who told Clarke of what he learned from Mr. Hubbard, Miss Rogers to whom all honor is due for her devoted work as first principal, but who would not have had the opportunity had not Mr. Hubbard discovered her—who might have found it hard during those first years to carry out her ideas had Mr. Hubbard not stood steadfastly by her side.

It was he and he alone who started the movement whose culmination was the Clarke School, he who drew up its charter, arranged all its legal business, organized the school and stayed by it through personal inconvenience until it was safe. To the last year of his life he remained one of its incorporators, traveling up there to attend its meetings and giving it the benefit of his advice. He did all this so quietly and simply that no one realized that it was anything of a sacrifice for an old man, as he came to be, to leave his comfortable home and many other interests to travel alone the long inconvenient distance between Washington and Northampton two or three times a year—just to help. He got no adequate thanks or recognition during his lifetime and he bids fair to get none now.

Understand I am not blaming anyone. Miss Rogers always tried to do him justice. Miss Yale is younger and has been too busy all her life trying to make the school the worthy memorial it is to have time to talk much about the past.

It is we, and especially I, who should have seen that his memory was adequately honored. True there is the Hubbard Hall, but that by itself is not enough. Anybody with enough money can have a hall named for him. What we need as a family is to cherish the Clarke School as one of our most precious heirlooms—a thing for us to be proud of and to take a personal interest in keeping it at the very top.

I do not see why Elsie should not be on the Board instead of you after this most critical year is passed. And if she does not feel a personal pride in it, if she does it simply as a matter of a disagreeable duty, I think she had better not touch it at all.

You talk of your children being the descendants of Alexander Graham Bell. They have a right to be proud for he is a fine man as well as a great one, but he is not the extent of their heritage. They also have their descent from the man who broke the spell that all children who could not hear were under at Hartford for fifty years. You have no conception of the horror that meant. It meant watching your child grow up without any education at all until she was twelve years old—then having to send her to what was a virtual prison, where she would remain six years, returning to you at eighteen educated after a fashion, but in such a way that she was almost as apart from you as when at Hartford, to remain so all your and her life.

My father saved me from that. So did Jennie Lippitt's mother save her, but that was all she did. Your children's great-grandfather did much more. He saved thousands and thousands of other fathers' children from that fate. Is that not a wonderful heritage to possess? Should it not be their great pride and ambition to see that the work he started should go on. Not only to go on, but to keep it as it is now at the top-most peak.

I have unburdened myself. I do not think it was so unnatural for me to feel as I did when I was in the arena. Now that my own personal fight is over, I do want to help the Clarke, my father's school, and I want my children and grandchildren who are perfectly normal to feel that its welfare is very near their hearts and to help in a very personal way.

I do not think you have ever realized before that there was any special reason why you should care particularly for Clarke and this has been my fault. This is why I am now trying to show you that there is a reason. It is not for Miss Yale's sake, praiseworthy as that motive may be, but for our family's honor.[6]

The following day, in a note to Elsie, she added:

I think the gist of the letter [to Bert] was that having taught you all my life to forget that I was deaf, I now want you to remember it, at least to the extent of looking on the Clarke School as a sort of family affair whose welfare is a family concern.[7]

Mabel's plea did not go unnoticed. To this day some member of her family has continued to serve on the Board of Trustees of the Clarke School.

240

20
The Closing Years

The passing years were beginning to take their toll. In 1921 Mabel, then in her sixty-fourth year, wrote Elsie:

I think Papa would be very pleased to meet Mr. and Mrs. Hoover at your dinner—but—I must ask you to leave us free to do as we like about coming.

Papa is very well—but he is older [seventy-four]—and so am I, and we can't recover from a journey as long as this as quickly as we used to. Papa wants to meet Einstein and others of the scientific men who come for the National Academy meeting on April 28th but he says he does not care to attend the meeting. I think he does not hear well enough to enjoy listening and I don't think he likes large dinner parties. He enjoyed Lord Bryce's lunch party [in Edinburgh], but it was rather a small affair, and that Papa enjoys more and appears to better advantage at a small rather than a large dinner. Too many people talking at once confuse him.[1]

Again writing to Elsie the same year:

I am sorry I have so little time to do more for you all. But Father demands more and more of me as he grows older and I want him to have all he wants. The great trouble is my time is very broken and I get tired.[2]

A letter written in 1919 addressed to "My Dear Children" was probably intended for both the Grosvenors and the Fairchilds:

The uncertainty of life is necessarily impressed upon one and before it is too late I want to write this letter to commend to your love and consideration Casey and Kathleen Baldwin and their children.

It is surely very unusual for one woman to be surrounded and brought into such intimate relationship with four such men as Father, Bert, David and Casey. Each is as free from mercenary thoughts as men can well be—and each is seeking the selfsame goal—the betterment of the world—and each is approaching that end from such absolutely different viewpoints. I have felt sometimes that they were all working so entirely apart from the others, like four separate worlds revolving around their own orbits. It was sometimes difficult for one or other to realize that the others truly are working with the best that is in them for that unselfish object. Only I, who am in the center and love them all, can see the truth and know that it is the truth, various as the means employed.

It goes without saying that your father has done a great deal for Casey. He has the opportunity and the power. Casey will always be the first to insist on his indebtedness. What may not be so obvious is that Casey himself has done his best to hold up his end—and he will always be the best to do that—it is for me to insist on it. He and Father have worked together all these years in harmony and single-mindedness seeking but to increase our knowledge of things that will be of benefit to mankind—and with no thought of pecuniary benefit. Casey has some small independent means and so has Kathleen—but I believe he is poorer than when he began to work with Father. He certainly has not profited in a monetary way—and my great concern now is what is to become of him and his family when Father and I go.

What I have to ask my heirs is this: He has been like a son to us all these years. He has had opportunities of helping us which Bert and David have not—and he has used those opportunities as Bert and David would have surely done.

I love him very dearly and Kathleen and the children—and I cannot bear to think that with Father and my going he may be turned out of home and place that has been his for so long....

I who love him commend him to you as a younger brother. Let him and Kathleen feel that you remember all that he has brought into your father's life that you would have brought had your interests been along the same lines. I am not making any bequest to them— that's not what I mean in writing this letter—only that you give them fellowship in your love for us and remembrance of us—and help them readjust their lives so that they will lose as little by our going as needs must.

I love you and trust you my children and think a mother was never more blessed than I have been in my daughters and sons-in-law.[3]

This same foreboding of the approaching end must have been with her when, a few months later in the same year, she wrote to Bert recalling a sight she had seen in China during their world tour in 1911:

Inspired by the great house of the greatest Dynasty of China at Mukden...there is a plain mound of earth unmarked, undecorated—just a plain, high mound on top of which in the course of centuries a fine tree has struggled for life, stunted, ragged, exposed to the northern winds. Here at last lies the Son of Heaven Celestial Ruler.

It has appealed to my imagination as no other grave has or can—and something of this is in my thoughts of our own grave. I would have our last resting place just as simple as that—marked only by the plainest identification marks—and the real, the big and lasting memorial elsewhere.[4]

Although the summer of 1922 found Alec in failing health, Mabel did not realize his life was ebbing away when she urged Elsie and Bert to carry out their plans for a trip to South America. However, she later shared her growing concern with her other son-in-law, David Fairchild:

Many thanks for your loving letter. As I telegraphed, we already tried to get our faithful Charles [Thompson], but of course, it would not be fair to urge him to come if his wife is seriously ill. I don't know of anyone else. A trained nurse wouldn't do as she would only annoy Daddysan and be a death's head at the table. He couldn't exchange sociabilities with the woman who discusses his insides—that isn't his kind. He is thin and white but Dr. Roy says there is no reason why he should not pull up and feel himself again—but I wonder—I understand better his limitations.

Last night he would not stay on the sofa but went to the piano and listened to Nancy Bell playing and to the gramophone played by Barbie, and Nancy Bell read to him quite a lot. So Daddysan and I and our granddaughters had a nice quiet evening together.[5]

And in this letter her sadness is apparent:

I have been unhappy about Daddysan—there was nothing very pleasant I could write of him. He does not gain and it is almost impossible to get him to take his medicine. Dr. Roy has been to see him twice and he sees no reason why Daddysan should not get over this anaemia, but he thinks it is a long way ahead. Meanwhile Daddysan spends most of his time dozing in bed. When he rouses himself, he is bright enough and he has been out every day.

I hope Daisy will come soon. Life is quiet enough here now—you would not know Beinn Bhreagh.[6]

The end came very quickly. On August 2, 1922, Mabel cabled to Bert:

Father died peacefully today. Only within a few days did we realize any danger. I did not send for David and Daisy. They were here by merest chance.[7]

Realizing how distressed Elsie must feel at being so far away, Daisy sent her this description of what took place at Beinn Bhreagh:

As far as Daddysan was concerned, one could not wish for a more beautiful ending. He was in the porch with the fresh air about him and it was a beautiful moonlight night and not cold. "How beautiful it is here—the air is so fresh," he said in the afternoon and he just breathed more deeply and more slowly until finally he didn't breathe again. He pressed Mother's hand almost to the end—and very shortly before he died when Mother was calling him, he opened his eyes and we all knew he had come back and knew her. I am sure Mother told you that—I think it was her greatest comfort.

I don't think you need fear that Mother will break down now anyway. It makes you cry to see her. She goes on just as usual—makes all the motion— laughs and talks but you never forget for a moment that the heart of everything has gone out of life for her forever.

She isn't wearing mourning. She says she could never take it off if she did, she couldn't help watching us for the first signs of our putting it off. It would seem like putting off our sorrow. Up here, it has seemed so natural and so beautiful an ending. There was no crepe on the door—no drawn blinds—the children played about and ran up and down stairs—there was no feeling at all that death was terrible.

The men in the Laboratory made the coffin out of good rugged pine and forged the iron handles. It was lined with aeroplane linen. The children made a pall of green, entirely covered with balsam fir. They cut the branches very short and sewed them on. If you had seen them fitting it over the coffin themselves and doing it so sweetly and seriously, so glad there was something they could do for Grampie, you would be thankful for them that death can never seem a thing to fear.

The only flowers on the coffin were from the American Tel and Tel Company. The wreath must have been chosen by someone "with tenderness and imagination" Mother feels. It was made of laurel, sheaves of wheat and pink roses and Mother feels they were chosen—"the laurel for victory, the wheat for the gathered harvest and the roses for gentleness and sweetness."

Mother stepped forward and stood alone with her arm resting on the coffin—bare-headed and in white with a soft white scarf around her neck while the Rev. John MacKinnon read a few verses from the 90th Psalm—just the beautiful ones, skipping the others. Miss Jean MacDonald sang "Where Grew a Bonnie Briar Bush" and then played Mendelssohn's funeral march as they carried him out. John was there with the buckboard, the two back seats removed—and Mother, Mabel [Grosvenor] and I with the others behind watched them around the curve. It was a thrilling sight—Casey and Graham [Fairchild] walking at the head of twenty or thirty men—all bare-headed—then John with the buckboard with its fir-covered load.

Catherine [MacKenzie] drove Mother, Mabel, David, Nancy Bell and me—and the others followed in other cars. Mother had wanted to walk up beside the buckboard but we persuaded her it was too dangerous up the steep part. At the top of the mountain where the road merges from the woods, she got out and walked the rest of the way—David holding her arm. She walked on the right, her left hand on the coffin. Where the road leads straight to the circle, we all got out and followed on foot.

There were a great many people there. The grave was blasted out of the rock and lined with fir boughs—and there was a steel vault—in case Mother feels she wants Father to go back to America. On the

247

right the American flag and on the left the British were at half mast on short poles. Miss MacDonald sang the verses and we all joined in singing the chorus of "Bringing in the Sheaves." Mother watched Miss Mac-Donald's face and joined in first of all. Miss MacDonald's voice is beautiful and she sang so that every word was understood. She sang right to Mother. Then she sang Tennyson's "Crossing the Bar," then the first verse only of Stevenson's requiem:

"Under the wide and starry sky,
Dig the grave and let me lie,
Gladly I lived and gladly I die,
And I lay me down with a will."

The music of it is as beautiful as the words and as she sang, we looked over the beautiful stretch of water and hills and sky and it was gray and misty as Father loved it best.

Mr. MacKinnon read a few words Mother had written explaining that she wanted Longfellow's "Psalm of Life" read because it typified as could no mere personal words the spirit in which Dr. Bell had lived his life, and then Mr. MacKinnon read it and after that we all said the "Lord's Prayer" and the coffin was lowered into the grave. "Lord, now lettest thou thy servant depart in peace. May the peace of God that passeth all understanding be with you and remain with you always, amen."

Uncle Charlie [Bell] wonders if any other great man ever had so simple a funeral. I wish you could have been there on the mountain Elsie, darling, and Bert and all your children and everyone who loved

Daddysan. It was Mother's planning and Mother's idea that made it like a last message from Daddysan. There was nothing that did not ring absolutely true, there was no pretence of any kind, no show.

I don't believe Mother will ever want Father moved from here. I hope not, but that doesn't need to be decided now—and I know she wants to talk to you. Just now Mother wants to sell the Washington house without ever seeing it again. If Casey can find his life's still here, Mother can go on living here too—going away of course in the winter and keeping the home for us all in the summer. So far there seems no reason why this will not work out.[8]

As soon as Bert and Elsie returned from South America, they went directly to Beinn Bhreagh. Bert then left for Washington, taking some of the children back to school, while Elsie and the younger ones remained with her mother. In the meantime, Mabel endeavored to gather herself together, and wrote to Bert to this effect:

There is one thing that makes it very hard for me to discuss things—and it is that for forty-five years I have lived with a very silent man. He rarely discussed things and hated arguments—and I could hardly ever get him to tell me what he thought of things.

Now I hold myself as his representative. My chief business is not to talk any more than I can help but to try to carry out his wishes so far as I think I know them. But there are several things which I cannot carry out without your help and David's and Casey's.

You are the one to whom I must look especially for help on the biography that must be written and I want above all things to have you tell me your ideas. Also, I want you always to feel that you can speak to me freely about anything and that I am glad to have you do so—even although I may not agree. Even when I go against your suggestions, it won't be because I have not considered them—only that after thinking them over, I decide that I prefer my own way.

When I do that, it is easier for me to just do it and not talk about it for that is the way Father brought me up. When he made up his mind, he did it without discussion and I always yielded without argument for I knew argument was of no use.

He did not talk—he simply did. I can't do that often but sometimes I can and I don't want you to think too badly of me for doing things of which your judgment disapproves. I love you always and have the very highest respect for your judgment in many things, but in some I much prefer my own.[9]

After her husband's death, Mabel's own health began to fail, and Elsie must have written to the family in Washington about it. Mabel wrote to Bert explaining:

Personally, I cannot see anything wrong with me, more than would be natural under the circumstances. It is hardly to be expected that a wife could be parted from her husband with perfect calmness and it is simply that I am coming more to the realization of things. When you were here, I was too busy to realize anything at all and could then do things impossible to me now.

I only want to be let alone. I have my hands full of things I want to do for Father and I have not much

energy, it takes a long time to get anything done.[10]

The *Home Notes*, a daily record of Bell's work and family life started by Bell in 1879 and continued by Mabel after his death, provides insight into the things she wanted "to do for Father." It was apparent that she had determined Beinn Bhreagh should continue to be the center for their extended family as it had been during Alec's lifetime.

The Fairchild family and a number of relatives who had come to attend Bell's funeral remained for a holiday at Beinn Bhreagh. In September they were joined by the Grosvenor family. Golf and fishing were always available to those who enjoyed it, and frequently Mabel accompanied family members who went sailing on the Bras d'Or Lakes. She was particularly delighted to observe how well the various grandchildren learned to sail the *Elsie*. On two occasions she organized a wilderness expedition to Garloch Mountain in search of the falls. Many invited guests joined their large family for meals. On on occasion Mabel extended an invitation to the wives of some visiting yachtmen to dine at Beinn Bhreagh Hall. Expecting eight, she discovered at the last minute that eighteen were coming. Quickly, the menu was changed and the table reset so that her guests were unaware of the error. Amid all this activity she made sure that the younger children were not overlooked, arranging a picnic for them.

In addition to her domestic arrangements she found time to think about how her husband's wishes could be carried out regarding his work with Baldwin on the hydrofoils. She felt certain that if arrangements were made for Baldwin to continue this work, in time the world would come to know the greatness of their achievement. She hoped that this, in turn, would bring fame and fortune to Casey.

I am giving much thought to what is to be done to give effect to Mr. Bell's last wishes—to carry on the H.D. work, to stand by Casey and look after Kathleen and the children.

I think favorably of the idea of endowing a sort of Research Laboratory to carry on experimental work in the old laboratory building here. This of course would depend on Mr. Baldwin's willingness to cooperate. The idea would be to set aside a certain sum—say sufficient to produce an income of $10,000 a year. This to be placed absolutely at Mr. Baldwin's disposal to be expended as he deems best in the furtherance of the work he and Mr. Bell talked about. If inventions of a practical nature were the result and money came from them, part could be devoted to making the endowment permanent so that a permanent Graham Bell Research Laboratory somewhat similar to the Rockefeller Institute [could be established]. How this is to be worked out is not clear, but I am clear that we must trust Mr. Baldwin implicitly.[11]

By September 6, 1922, her ideas had crystallized:

Mr. Baldwin and I have today signed a contract whereby we agree together that we will continue to carry on the work that Mr. Bell, Baldwin and I have been carrying on—so far as it is possible to do so without Mr. Bell. This agreement is to last for ten years and calls for an expenditure of $10,000 a year for experimental work to be at Baldwin's sole discretion. This I believe to be along the lines of Mr. Bell's wish

252

many times expressed. We hope it will be possible to make this experimental laboratory so successful that at the end of the ten-year period it will be so well established that it will be permanent without further financial help from the family.[12]

It was customary for Baldwin to describe in the *Home Notes* the experiments on which he was engaged. On October 4, 1922, Mabel made this entry:

I wish Mr. Baldwin would note here some of the problems he is encountering in his work—while I cannot discuss this as Mr. Bell did, I am interested to know what they are. If he would write them out so that I could read them later on I could ask questions that would help me in following Mr. Baldwin's work.[13]

Meantime, she was giving considerable thought to what should be done with the sheep:

Miss MacKenzie [Bell's secretary] is hard at work preparing the sheep book for the annual October weighing. It is not our intention at present to continue the sheep experiments of Mr. Bell's because we do not want to injure the record as we fear would be the case since there is no one who really cares about them....[14]

We propose to weigh the sheep as usual on October 1st, selection as directed by Mr. Bell and mating with Davidson's ram. We will care for the flock as usual this winter and try and see if we can find an intelligent and practical man who would like to go on with the experiments and try to apply them to practical use....[15]

I spent most of the day yesterday, October 6th, struggling with the sheep problem. Although Mr. Bell insisted always on talking of "Mrs. Bell's multi-nippled flock," I never had anything more to do with it than expressing the general wish that a twin-bearing stock be established, that being the object Mr. Bell had before him when he commenced sheep experiments in the 1880s.

I have therefore everything to learn of the general principles guiding Mr. Bell in the selection of his ewes. I want loyally to follow his principles but do not feel it necessary to blindly follow his procedure in detail, if after studying the matter, I think he would himself change it. [16]

Mabel wished that members of her family would contribute to the endowment fund for the Clarke School for the Deaf to commemorate the work accomplished by her father and husband. She wrote a number of letters, similar to the one written earlier to Bert, urging them to assume a personal responsibility in maintaining the high standard of the Clarke School for the Deaf. She received a letter from Miss Yale, the school's principal, asking her to take her husband's place on the Board of Trustees, and she accepted this position.

Her husband's biography was a matter of continuing concern, and she looked to Bert Grosvenor for help:

Had a long talk with Mr. Grosvenor yesterday, September 20th, about the biography, decided not to hurry, but continue to employ Mr. DeLand [who was employed by the National Geographic Society] for safe keeping at present. I will assume Mr. DeLand's salary so that his work will be my property. [17]

By November her health had seriously deteriorated.

Bert was anxious that some definite arrangement be made as quickly as possible for writing the Bell biography. He suggested that he go to London and discuss the subject with Lytton Strachey, whose recent book *Queen Victoria* established his reputation as the outstanding English biographer. Mabel was not enthusiastic:

I have had the suggestion that Strachey write a life [of Bell] made me by others independently, but I am not sure that I like it. Certainly I am not at present in favor of your running over to England to see him. My feeling would be to have someone want to write it from his own feeling of fascination. So far as appears, Strachey wrote *Queen Victoria* because the subject interested him, not because he was given the order. Now if we had Father's material edited someone might see its possibilities and do it for his own pleasure. This might or might not work out, but I don't see why we want to rush into print. It would look as if we thought Father's fame ephemeral and wanted to get all there was out of it.[18]

Elsie expressed increasing alarm over her mother's health when she wrote to Bert:

Mama is not well. She has no appetite and her food disturbs her when she eats it. Her symptoms are somewhat like Papa's. Please consult Dr. Foot and let me know. We cannot allow this condition to run on as Papa's did.[19]

A few days later she wrote:

Mama is much more reasonable than Papa ever was and really sometimes follows my advice. I hate to drag her away from here where she is occupied and

255

comparatively content too soon until after Christmas.

Mama had another flare-up two or three days ago but fortunately since then she has been willing to stay in bed and take a rest cure. Consequently, she looks better today. When I suggested it, to my surprise and delight, she agreed with me perfectly and said that she had too much to do to lie around half sick and if she didn't improve as fast as she ought, she promised me that she would pack up and come down to Washington to get matters attended to. She said that Papa's attitude of getting weaker and letting nature take its course and refusing to do anything worried her and that she did not intend to do that.[20]

Elsie and her mother returned to Washington in December. The doctors examined Mabel and found she was suffering from cancer. For the short time that remained she lived with Daisy. One day near the end, she remarked to her daughter: "Wasn't I clever not to get ill until Daddysan didn't need me any more."[21]

She died on January 3, 1923, at the age of sixty-five, and on August 7, in accordance with her expressed wish, her ashes were placed in her husband's grave on the summit of Beinn Bhreagh. With only the immediate family present, a brief service was conducted by the Reverend John MacKinnon.

The time chosen was five o'clock, the same hour as her husband's funeral a year earlier, the hour at which Mabel was accustomed to joining Alec at the laboratory to drive him home. It seemed fitting that all that was mortal of them should be together again in the place they loved so well.

Notes

Chapter 1—Early Childhood

1. Letters relating to Mabel Hubbard's childhood, Vol. 13, p.13.
2. Based on an address of A.G. Bell at the dedication of the Gardiner Greene Hubbard Memorial Hall, Clarke School for the Deaf, Feb. 1, 1913, B.B.R.
3. A.G. Bell in the B.B.R., Vol. 6, p. 43.
4. Recollections of Mary True, B.B.R., Vol. 24, p. 56.
5. Recollections of Mabel Hubbard's childhood, B.B.R., Vol. 23.
6. Helen E. Waite, *Make a Joyful Sound* (Philadelphia: MacRae, Smith Co., 1961).
7. Recollections of Mary True, B.B.R., Vol. 24, p. 56.

Chapter 2—Childhood in Europe

1. Journals of Mabel Hubbard, March 16, 1870-March 14, 1872, Vol. 103.
2. Journals of Mabel Hubbard, Vol. 103.
3. Mabel Hubbard's letters to her mother, Vol. 77.
4. Journals of Mabel Hubbard, Vol. 103.
5. Mabel Hubbard's letters to her mother, Vol. 77.
6. Journals of Mabel Hubbard, Vol. 103.
7. Journals of Mabel Hubbard, Vol. 103.
8. Journals of Mabel Hubbard, Vol. 104.
9. Journals of Mabel Hubbard, Vol. 104.
10. Journals of Mabel Hubbard, Vol. 104.

11. Journals of Mabel Hubbard, Vol. 104.

Chapter 3—Mabel's Encounter with Bell

1. Reminiscences of early days of speech teaching, A.G. Bell in the B.B.R., Vol. 12, p. 171.
2. Journals of Mabel Hubbard, Jan. 1879.
3. Letter of Mabel Hubbard to her mother, Vol. 78.
4. Letter of Mabel Hubbard to her mother, Vol. 78.
5. Letter of Mabel Hubbard to her mother, Vol. 78.
6. Letter of Mabel Hubbard to her mother, Vol. 78.
7. Journals of Mabel Hubbard, 1874.

Chapter 4—The Engagement

1. Mrs. Hubbard to Mr. Hubbard, Feb. 14, 1874.
2. A.G. Bell to Mrs. Hubbard, June 24, 1875.
3. Mabel Hubbard to Mrs. Hubbard, Aug. 2, 1875.
4. A.G. Bell to Mr. and Mrs. Hubbard, Aug. 5, 1875.
5. Letters relating to the marriage of Mabel Hubbard and A.G. Bell, Vol. 123.

Chapter 5—Courtship

1. Mabel Hubbard to A.G. Bell, Nov. 26, 1875.
2. Mabel Hubbard to A.G. Bell, Dec. 1875.
3. A.G. Bell to Mabel Hubbard, Nov. 1876.
4. Mabel Hubbard to A.G. Bell, June 19, 1876.
5. Mabel Hubbard to A.G. Bell, July 26, 1876.
6. A.G. Bell to Mabel Hubbard, June 18, 1876.
7. Mabel Hubbard to A.G. Bell, June 24, 1876.
8. Mabel Hubbard to A.G. Bell, June 18, 1876.
9. Mabel Hubbard to A.G. Bell, Aug. 1876.
10. Mabel Hubbard to A.G. Bell, Aug. 2, 1876.

11. Mabel Hubbard to A.G. Bell, 1875.

12. Mabel Hubbard to A.G. Bell, 1875.

13. A. G. Bell to Mabel Hubbard, Jan. 1876.

14. A. G. Bell to Mabel Hubbard, Jan. 1876.

15. Mabel Hubbard to A.G. Bell, Jan. 18, 1876.

16. Mabel Hubbard to A.G. Bell, Nov. 9, 1876.

17. Mabel Hubbard to A.G. Bell, Nov. 12, 1876.

18. Mabel Hubbard to A.G. Bell, Nov. 1876.

19. Mabel Hubbard to A.G. Bell, Dec. 3, 1876.

20. Mabel Hubbard to A.G. Bell, Jan. 18, 1877.

21. Mabel Hubbard to A.G. Bell, April 7, 1877.

22. Robert V. Bruce, *Alexander Graham Bell: The Conquest of Solitude* (Boston: Little, Brown & Co., 1973), p. 233.

Chapter 6—First Year of Marriage

1. Mabel Hubbard to Mrs. Hubbard, July 20, 1877.

2. Mabel Hubbard to Mrs. Hubbard, Aug. 11, 1877.

3. Mabel Hubbard to Mrs. Hubbard, Aug. 15, 1877.

4. Mabel Hubbard to Mrs. Hubbard, Sept. 27, 1877.

5. Mabel Hubbard to Mrs. Hubbard, Sept. 27, 1877.

6. Mabel Hubbard to Mrs. Hubbard, Oct. 8, 1877.

7. Mabel Hubbard to Mrs. Hubbard, 1877.

8. Mabel Hubbard to Mrs. Hubbard, Dec. 26, 1877.

9. Mabel Hubbard to Mrs. Hubbard, Nov. 10, 1877.

10. Mabel Hubbard to Mrs. Hubbard, Dec. 11, 1877.

11. Mabel Hubbard to Mrs. Hubbard, Nov. 10, 1877.

12. Mabel Hubbard to Mrs. Hubbard, 1877.

13. Mabel Hubbard to Mrs. Hubbard, Jan. 4, 1878.

14. Mabel Hubbard to Mrs. Hubbard, Jan. 4, 1878.

15. Mabel Hubbard to Mrs. Hubbard, Jan. 9, 1878.

16. Mabel Hubbard to Mrs. Hubbard, Feb. 26, 1878.
17. A.G. Bell to Mrs. Hubbard, Feb. 21, 1878.
18. Mrs. Hubbard to Mrs. Melville Bell, April 17, 1878.
19. A.G. Bell to Mr. and Mrs. Melville Bell, Sept. 1878.

Chapter 7—Storm Clouds

1. Mabel Bell to Mrs. Hubbard, Nov. 21, 1877.
2. Mabel Bell to Mrs. Hubbard, Dec. 11, 1877.
3. Mabel Bell to Mrs. Hubbard, Dec. 26, 1877.
4. Mabel Bell to Mrs. Hubbard, Dec. 26, 1877.
5. Catherine Mackenzie, *Alexander Graham Bell: The Man Who Contracted Space* (Boston: Houghton Mifflin Co., 1928), p. 200.
6. Mabel Bell to A.G. Bell, Aug. 16, 1878.
7. A.G. Bell to Mabel Bell, Aug. 21, 1878.
8. A.G. Bell to Mabel Bell, Sept. 9, 1878.
9. Mabel Bell to Mrs. Hubbard, Nov. 1878.

Chapter 8—Return to the United States

1. A.G. Bell to Mabel Bell, March 1879.
2. Journals of Mabel Bell, March 1879.
3. A.G. Bell to Mabel Bell, March 1879.
4. Journals of Mabel Bell, March 1879.
5. Journals of Mabel Bell, Aug. 12, 1879.
6. Mabel Bell to Mrs. Hubbard, March 11, 1879.
7. Journals of Mabel Bell, Feb. 23, 1879.
8. Journals of Mabel Bell, Feb. 14, 1879.
9. Journals of Mabel Bell, Feb. 12, 1879.
10. A.G. Bell to Mabel Bell, Jan. 11, 1879.
11. Mabel Bell to A.G. Bell, March 9, 1879.
12. Mabel Bell to A.G. Bell, March 20, 1879.

13. A.G. Bell to Mabel Bell, 1879.

14. Journals of Mabel Bell, March 1879.

15. Journals of Mabel Bell, Aug. 12, 1879.

16. Mabel Bell to Mrs. Melville Bell, Dec. 14, 1879.

17. Mabel Bell to Mrs. Melville Bell, Jan. 20, 1880.

18. Mabel Bell to Mrs. Melville Bell, Feb. 1880.

19. Mabel Bell to A.G. Bell, April 25, 1879.

20. Mabel Bell to Mrs. Hubbard, July 5, 1879.

21. Mabel Bell to A.G. Bell, June 19, 1880.

Chapter 9—Family Life

1. Mabel Bell to Mrs. Hubbard, June 1881.

2. Mabel Bell to Mrs. Hubbard, July 5, 1881.

3. Mabel Bell to Mrs. Melville Bell, July 17, 1881.

4. Mabel Bell to A.G. Bell, July 16, 1881.

5. Mabel Bell to A.G. Bell, July 29, 1881.

6. Mabel Bell to A.G. Bell, Aug. 1, 1881.

7. Mabel Bell to A.G. Bell, Aug. 26, 1882.

8. Mabel Bell to Mrs. Melville Bell, Sept. 1881.

9. Mabel Bell to Mrs. Hubbard, April 9, 1882.

10. Mabel Bell to Mrs. Hubbard, June 1882.

11. Journals of Mabel Bell, Feb. 1884.

12. Journals of Mabel Bell, Oct. 25, 1884.

13. Journals of Mabel Bell, June 18, 1885.

14. Journals of Mabel Bell, Nov. 14, 1884.

15. Journals of Mabel Bell, Nov. 21, 1886.

16. Journals of Mabel Bell, Sept. 1885.

17. A.G. Bell to Mabel Bell, June 16, 1885.

18. Journals of Mabel Bell, Oct. 25, 1884.

19. A.G. Bell to Mabel Bell, May 23, 1887.

20. Journals of Mabel Bell, Oct. 25, 1884.

Chapter 10—Discovering Baddeck

1. Mabel Bell to Mrs. Hubbard, Sept. 1885.
2. Recollections prepared for the A.G. Bell Club by Maud Dunlop MacKenzie.
3. Journals of Mabel Bell, Sept. 17, 1885.
4. Mabel Bell to Mrs. Hubbard, Aug. 14, 1885.
5. Mabel Bell to Mrs. Hubbard, Aug. 20, 1886.
6. Mabel Bell to Mrs. Hubbard, Aug. 29, 1886.
7. Mabel Bell to Mrs. Hubbard, Aug. 1, 1886.
8. Mabel Bell to Mrs. Hubbard, Aug. 20, 1886.
9. Mabel Bell to Mrs. Hubbard, Sept. 1, 1890.
10. Mabel Bell to Mrs. Hubbard, Oct. 12, 1890.
11. Mabel Bell to Mrs. Hubbard, Oct. 19, 1890.
12. Mabel Bell to Mrs. Hubbard, Nov. 2, 1890.
13. "Memories of Dr. and Mrs. Bell," by Mrs. David Fairchild, Vol. 174.
14. Mabel Bell to Mrs. Hubbard, Dec. 11, 1890.
15. Mabel Bell to Mrs. Hubbard, Dec. 1890.
16. "Memories of Dr. and Mrs. Bell," by Mrs. David Fairchild, Vol. 174.

Chapter 11—Life is Not Simple

1. Journals of Mabel Bell, Oct. 25, 1885.
2. Journals of Mabel Bell, Nov. 19, 1885.
3. Mabel Bell to A.G. Bell, May 28, 1894.
4. Mabel Bell to A.G. Bell, July 1883.
5. Journals of Mabel Bell, June 30, 1887.
6. Journals of Mabel Bell, Sept. 1885.
7. Mabel Bell to A.G. Bell, June 30, 1883.
8. Mabel Bell to A.G. Bell, June 18, 1888.
9. A.G. Bell to Mabel Bell, June 29, 1888.

10. Mabel Bell to A.G. Bell, July 11, 1884.

11. A. G. Bell to Mabel Bell, May 25, 1887.

12. Mabel Bell to Mrs. Hubbard, Sept. 17, 1890.

13. Mabel Bell to Mrs. Hubbard, Sept. 30, 1890.

14. Mabel Bell to A.G. Bell, Jan. 18, 1891.

15. Mabel Bell to A.G. Bell, Dec. 1891.

16. Mabel Bell to A.G. Bell, June 27, 1888.

17. A. G. Bell to Mabel Bell, June 24, 1889.

Chapter 12—Life at Beinn Bhreagh

1. Mabel Bell to A.G. Bell, April 29, 1891.

2. Mabel Bell to Elsie Bell, undated.

3. Letters of Mary Blatchford, B.B.R., Vol. 23.

4. Letters of Mary Blatchford, B.B.R., Vol. 23.

5. Mabel Bell to Daisy Bell, Oct. 1897.

6. Lord Kelvin to Mabel Bell, April 20, 1898.

7. Mabel Bell to A.G. Bell, Jan. 21, 1895.

8. Mabel Bell to A.G. Bell, June 1893.

9. A.G. Bell to Mabel Bell, Jan. 7, 1892.

Chapter 13—Their Daughters' Romances

1. Mabel Bell to A.G. Bell, May 12, 1895.

2. Mabel Bell to A.G. Bell, May 24, 1895.

3. Mabel Bell to A.G. Bell, May 25, 1895.

4. Mabel Bell to A.G. Bell, June 2, 1895.

5. Mabel Bell to A.G. Bell, June 2, 1895.

6. Mabel Bell to A.G. Bell, June 25, 1895.

7. Mabel Bell to A.G. Bell, June 26, 1895.

8. Mabel Bell to A.G. Bell, Nov. 14, 1899.

9. Mabel Bell to A.G. Bell, March 10, 1896.

10. Mabel Bell to A.G. Bell, March 23, 1896.

11. Mabel Bell to A.G. Bell, Nov. 5, 1896.

12. Mabel Bell to A.G. Bell, Nov. 23, 1896.

13. Mabel Bell to Daisy Bell, Nov. 1896.

14. Mabel Bell to Daisy Bell, Dec. 1896.

15. Mabel Bell to A.G. Bell, June 1, 1897.

16. Mabel Bell to A.G. Bell, May 12, 1899.

17. Mabel Bell to Elsie Bell, Spring 1898.

18. A.G. Bell to Mabel Bell, May 25, 1899.

19. Mabel Bell to A.G. Bell, May 29, 1899.

20. Mabel Bell to Mrs. Kennan, Sept. 30, 1900.

21. Mabel Bell to Mrs. Kennan, Nov. 4, 1900.

22. Mabel Bell to Daisy Bell, 1900.

23. A.G. Bell to Mabel Bell, June 8, 1898.

24. Mabel Bell to Elsie Bell, June 1898.

25. Mabel Bell to Daisy Bell, May 18, 1904.

26. Mabel Bell to Daisy Bell, Oct. 24, 1904.

27. Mabel Bell to Daisy Bell, Oct. 26, 1904.

28. Mabel Bell to Mrs. Hubbard, Aug. 1907.

Chapter 14—The Mature Mabel

1. Mabel Bell to Mrs. Kennan, Dec. 1897.

2. Mabel Bell to Mrs. Kennan, Dec. 26, 1897.

3. Mabel Bell to A.G. Bell, June 1898.

4. Mabel Bell to Miss Caroline McCurdy, May 15, 1898.

5. Mabel Bell to Mrs. Hubbard, undated, 1898.

6. Mabel Bell to Mrs. Kennan, Jan. 22, 1898.

7. Mabel Bell to A.G. Bell, May 12, 1903.

8. Mabel Bell to A.G. Bell, Jan.12, 1898.

9. Mabel Bell to Mrs. Hubbard, Nov. 1897.

10. A.G. Bell to Mabel Bell, June 5, 1899.

11. Mabel Bell to A.G. Bell, Oct. 10, 1901.

12. *Home Notes*, Nov. 18, 1902.

13. Mabel Bell to Gilbert Grosvenor, Nov. 24, 1905.

Chapter 15—The Aerial Experiment Association

1. Mabel Bell to Daisy Fairchild, Nov. 1906.

2. Mabel Bell to Mrs. Hubbard, Nov. 1907.

3. H. Gordon Green, *The Silver Dart* (Fredericton, N.B.: Brunswick Press Ltd., 1959), p. 40.

4. Mabel Bell to Daisy Fairchild, June 1908.

5. Daisy Fairchild to Dr. and Mrs. A.G. Bell, *A.E.A. Bulletin*, Vol. 13, p. 16.

6. David Fairchild, *The World Was My Garden* (New York: Charles Scribner's & Sons Ltd., 1945), p. 344.

7. Mabel Bell to A.G. Bell, Sept. 17, 1908.

8. Mabel Bell to Daisy Fairchild, Feb. 23, 1909.

9. Mabel Bell to Daisy Fairchild, Feb. 24, 1909.

10. Mabel Bell to A.G. Bell, March 1909.

11. Casey Baldwin writing in the *A.E.A. Bulletin*, Vol. 36, p. 50.

12. Telegram, A.G. Bell to Glenn Curtiss, March 1909.

13. Glenn Curtiss to A.G. Bell, March 1909.

14. Telegram, A.G. Bell to Glenn Curtiss, March 1909.

15. *A.E.A. Bulletin*, Vol. 39, p. 1, March 31, 1909.

Chapter 16—The Intervening Years

1. Mabel Bell to A.G. Bell, Spring 1906.

2. Mabel Bell to A.G. Bell, March 20, 1909.

3. Mabel Bell to A.G. Bell, April 1909.

4. Mabel Bell to Mrs. Hubbard, Aug. 1909.

5. Mabel Bell to Daisy Fairchild, Aug. 1909.

6. Mabel Bell to A.G. Bell, Nov. 8, 1909.

7. Mabel Bell to A.G. Bell, Nov. 15, 1909.

8. Mabel Bell to Miss Yale, Nov. 14, 1909.

9. Mabel Bell to Daisy Fairchild, March 13, 1910.

10. B.B.R., 1910.

11. Mabel Bell to Elsie Grosvenor, March 17, 1911.

12. Mabel Bell to Daisy Fairchild, Nov. 4, 1914.

13. Mabel Bell to Daisy Fairchild, undated.

14. Mabel Bell to Daisy Fairchild, Aug. 2, 1916.

15. Mabel Bell to Daisy Fairchild, June 24, 1917.

16. Mabel Bell to Daisy Fairchild, July 5, 1917.

17. *Home Notes*, Vol. 106.

18. Mabel Bell to Daisy Fairchild, June 29, 1917.

19. Mabel Bell to A.G. Bell, April 15, 1917.

20. Mabel Bell to A.G. Bell, April 16, 1917.

21. Appeal written by Mabel Bell, April 1917.

22. Mabel Bell to A.G. Bell, April 25, 1917.

23. J.H. Parkin, *Bell and Baldwin* (Toronto: University of Toronto Press, 1964), p. 429.

Chapter 17—A Forgotten Page of History

1. Mabel Bell to Daisy Fairchild, 1906.

2. Mabel Bell to Daisy and David Fairchild, Sept. 1, 1908.

3. Mabel Bell to David Fairchild, April 1919.

4. J.H. Parkin, *Bell and Baldwin* (Toronto: University of Toronto Press, 1964), p. 426.

Chapter 18—Mabel's Grandchildren and the Montessori System

1. *Home Notes*, Sept. 23, 1902.

2. Mabel Bell to Gilbert Grosvenor, July 1905.

3. Mabel Bell to A.G. Bell, Aug. 21, 1906.

4. Mabel Bell to David Fairchild, Oct. 1, 1921.

5. Mabel Bell to Gilbert Grosvenor, Oct. 16, 1914.

6. Mabel Bell to Elsie Grosvenor, undated.

7. Mabel Bell to David Fairchild, Aug. 5, 1917.

8. "Dr. Montessori's Visit to America," by Marian Fairchild, in the B.B.R., Vol. 5, p. 145.

9. Mabel Bell to Mrs. Kennan, Oct. 1, 1913.

Chapter 19—Life in Retrospect

1. Mabel Bell to David Fairchild, Oct. 31, 1911.

2. Mabel Bell to Gilbert Grosvenor, Feb. 10, 1920.

3. Mabel Bell to Gilbert Grosvenor, 1915.

4. Mabel Bell to Gilbert Grosvenor, Nov. 5, 1915.

5. Mabel Bell to Gilbert Grosvenor, May 4, 1922.

6. Mabel Bell to Gilbert Grosvenor, Oct. 11, 1921.

7. Mabel Bell to Elsie Grosvenor, Oct. 12, 1921.

Chapter 20—The Closing Years

1. Mabel Bell to Elsic Grosvenor, 1921.

2. Mabel Bell to Elsie Grosvenor, Feb. 23, 1921.

3. Mabel Bell, letter to "Dear Children," Jan. 22, 1919.

4. Mabel Bell to Gilbert Grosvenor, April 4, 1919.

5. Mabel Bell to David Fairchild, July 1922.

6. Mabel Bell to David Fairchild, July 17, 1922.

7. Mabel Bell to Gilbert Grosvenor, Aug. 2, 1922.

8. Daisy Fairchild to Elsie Grosvenor, Aug. 6, 1922.

9. Mabel Bell to Gilbert Grosvenor, Sept. 19, 1922.

10. Mabel Bell to Gilbert Grosvenor, Nov. 11, 1922.

11. *Home Notes*.

12. *Home Notes*, Sept. 6, 1922.

13. *Home Notes*, Oct. 4, 1922.

14. *Home Notes*.

15. *Home Notes*.

16. *Home Notes*.

17. *Home Notes*, Sept. 21, 1922.

18. *Home Notes*, Nov. 1922.

19. Elsie Grosvenor to Gilbert Grosvenor, Nov. 5, 1922.

20. Elsie Grosvenor to Gilbert Grosvenor, Nov. 11, 1922.

21. Recollections of Daisy Fairchild.

Bibliography

Bruce, Robert V. *Alexander Graham Bell: The Conquest of Solitude*. Boston: Little, Brown & Co., 1973.

Fairchild, David. *The World Was My Garden*. New York: Charles Scribner's & Sons Ltd., 1945.

Green, H. Gordon. *The Silver Dart*. Fredericton, N.B.: Brunswick Press Ltd., 1959.

Lesage, the Hon. Jean. "Alexander Graham Bell Museum: Tribute to Genius," in the *National Geographic* magazine, August 1956.

Lillard, Paula Polk. *Montessori: A Modern Approach*. New York: Schocken Books, Inc., 1973.

Mackenzie, Catherine. *Alexander Graham Bell: The Man Who Contracted Space*. Boston: Houghton Mifflin Co., 1928.

Montessori, Maria. *The Montessori Method*. Anne E. George, trans. Cambridge, Mass.: R. Bentley, 1965.

Orem, R.C. *Montessori Today*. Toronto: Longmans Canada Ltd., 1971.

Parkin, J.H. *Bell and Baldwin*. Toronto: University of Toronto Press, 1964.

Roseberry, Cecil. *Glenn Curtiss: Pioneer of Flight*. Garden City, N.Y.: Doubleday, 1972.

Standing, E.M. *Maria Montessori*. New York: New American Library, 1957.

Waite, Helen E. *Make a Joyful Sound*. Philadelphia: MacRae, Smith Co., 1961.

Source Material:
A.E.A. Bulletin
Beinn Bhreagh Recorder
Home Notes
Journals of Mabel Hubbard Bell
Letters of Mabel Hubbard Bell
Letters of Alexander Graham Bell
Letters of Mrs. G.G. Hubbard
Files of the Alexander Graham Bell Club

ALSO AVAILABLE FROM
Breton Books and Music

• CAPE BRETON WORKS
More Lives from *Cape Breton's Magazine*

From farm life to boxing, from lighthouse tragedies to fishing adventures, from hunting to mining with horses to work in the steel plant—this extraordinary mix of men's and women's lives delivers a solid dose of the tenacity, courage, humour and good storytelling that make a place like Cape Breton work. **$23.50**

• THE SEVEN-HEADED BEAST
**& Other Acadian Tales from Cape Breton Island
collected by Anselme Chiasson
translated by Rosie Aucoin Grace**

These passionate, funny, bawdy and tender tales draw us closer to the heart of Acadian Cape Breton. Here's lively translations from the French of traditional storytellers Marcellin Haché and Loubie Chiasson, plus an introduction to their native Cheticamp by Père Anselme Chiasson.
$16.25

• THE GLACE BAY MINERS' MUSEUM
by Sheldon Currie

While the ending of this book is shattering and unforgettable, Sheldon Currie's real contribution is excellent storytelling and the remarkable Margaret, an indelible new voice in Canadian literature. A passionate and compassionate novel set in the coal life of Cape Breton Island, this is a story that will reverberate and last. It is also a bizarre and marvelous book! **$16.25**

continued on next page . . .